PRAYERS THAT AVAIL

By Beatrice Omojole

DEDICATION

I dedicate this book to my ever-faithful friend, comforter, helper and voice of sound reasoning; the Holy Spirit. It is simply because of your inspiration and tutelage that I have something to share with others. I therefore dedicate this book to you.

Thank YOU!

With love,

Your Girl Bea

ACKNOWLEDGEMENTS

Writing a book is harder than I thought and more rewarding than I could have ever imagined. None of this would have ever been possible without the help of the Holy Spirit. He was the first friend that read through this book. He stood by me during all my struggles and all my successes. He is the reason this book can be read aloud today.

"I have to start by thanking my dear big brother, mentor and friend Mr. Segun Ajala, from reading early drafts to giving me advice on my content and structure of this book, down to imparting me with spirit filled prayers; you were a key factor to this book getting started. Thank you so much.

I'm again thankful to Accelerated Authors Academy and Pastor Tunji Olujimi for their help in publishing this book. To all the editorial and proofreading team's attention to detail, keen insight, and support in bringing this book to life. It is because of their efforts and expertise that I have a legacy to leave behind and pass on to my generation and beyond.

To my family, my four pillars, for always being the ones I could turn to at every moment in my life, to my amazing Mother and Father Mr & Mrs Omojole, thank you for your effectual prayers over me and your unwavering love and support. To my sisters, Mary and Priscilla; thank you for lending your ears and being my human thesaurus every time I ask which word or phrase sounds better, I am really grateful to have you both as my beautiful sisters.

Finally, to all those who have been a part of my amazing journey, thank you all so very much.

PREFACE

As I write on this topic, I begin to understand the importance and significance of its existence. Today prayer is slowly losing its crucial place in our society, our churches, our marriages, our families and even down into our hearts.

From my experiences growing up in this generation and even at this present time, I believe prayer has become inconsequential. It is something which is talked about and mentioned, but not fully understood. It is merely skimmed over, now a commonly used phrase; we see it all the time on social media as a generic word or emoji when a national crisis happens. Prayer has been reduced to hashtags and nice things to say when we want to wish someone well or encourage them through a particular situation. Often, we tell those in need I'll pray for you; saying things like 'prayers going up for you' without ever uttering any words from our lips. Don't get me wrong, these things are great and in the time of crisis when people do pray, we can definitely see the effects and results from it. Just imagine if we did this all the time and we committed to praying consistently for ourselves, families, friends and our nations. There is no telling the miracles, signs and wonders we could experience here on earth.

The value of prayer is uncontested and can be the difference between life and death. The depth and height to which prayer reaches is invaluable and it simply cannot be measured. My experience of life so far has taught me the importance and significance of prayers. Prayer is not just what my life has been built upon but is the very reason why I am here and pressing forward in Jesus Christ each and every day.

The fact that prayer is mentioned is positive, however there is so much more to it, simply mentioning prayer, thinking of prayer or merely reciting religious words is not enough. It is time for the bride of Christ to know how to be effective in the place of prayer and activate its full power. This is one of the tools God has given us to communicate, shape and mould our destinies in alignment with His will.

My desire is that this becomes one of your most frequently and efficiently used tools too.

I hope you enjoy your reading.

Beatrice Omojole

CONTENTS

INTRODUCTION:
THE PURPOSE

'THE PRAYER OF A RIGHTEOUS WOMAN AVAILETH MUCH!' I heard those words as a still small voice in my ear as if I had been playing a game of Chinese whispers, the advantage here is that I had been selected as the first to hear the words and now I could pass it on clearly. As I lay in bed almost drifting to sleep and heard those words, I knew in that moment that this was a title of a book, but not just any book, a book that I needed to write.

It was the night of 16th April 2018; I remember the night well because earlier that day I had spoken on the topic of holiness at my church, by the evening, the effect of the day had started to take its toll on me. There I was stretched out across my bed, exhausted, waiting to drift to sleep but before I could, I fell into a trance, conscious of where I was but captivated by a strong and powerful presence. The moment could not have lasted longer than a minute in real time, but the message was timeless. I always like to think of it as God pressing pause on time just so He could speak to me. I knew when I heard and saw those words in my mind that this was from God.

In the weeks and months following this divine encounter, God started taking me through a journey of discovery and purpose. I'll gently warn you now, if God decides to take you on a journey, well, expect the unexpected and be sure to get buckled up because it is more likely to be a bumpy ride; that's not to say God is unsafe and unsure with where He is taking us. It gets bumpy because we tend to have a tantrum; kicking, screaming, protesting and taking some detours, well at least this was the case in my situation. However, along this adventurous journey, God taught me what the prayer of a righteous woman can do and how that can change the course and even the experience of our journeys. I will not pretend that this journey is always easy, and I won't start by telling you that it is, because that would be untrue but what I gained through my experiences is that it simultaneously challenged the core of who I am and transformed me into the best version of myself to date.

The answers and the solutions we are desperately searching for has already been given to us. In Acts 1:8 it says *But you shall receive power when the Holy Spirit comes upon you...'*

When you accept Jesus as your Lord and personal saviour, you also receive the Holy Spirit who governs and guides your spirit-being here on earth. This Holy Spirit doesn't just come into our lives ineffectively, but comes with power and authority. This is our birth right when we become born again by the spirit of God; we are also reborn with His power and His authority. It is readily available for you to use and explore. I write these words as an expression of God's heart to sharpen and refine the tool of prayer given to every believer and also to those who are unsure or have never heard about the effectual power of prayer. Time has passed since the idea of this book was birthed, since then many new revelations, encounters and insights into prayer have been uncovered. It is out of these discoveries, that I share my insight on what I have learned thus far. My prayer is that this book would uncover the power you hold within you to PRAY.

WHAT IS PRAYER?

Prayer is simply communication and the process by which a dialogue is created between man and God. Communication as we know it is an extremely broad term. Depending on the person you are communicating with, linguistic styles, tones and expressions may vary. Most of our interaction with others requires communication of some form, so that we can express ourselves in a verbal or non-verbal way. Communication is one of the main ingredients for success in everything that we do. If we do not communicate at all, it's actually impossible for us to achieve much or do anything. The better we communicate with others, the better the results we receive; this is true in any case, whether in marriage, parenting, friends and in our careers.

With most CV's and job profiles, it's almost guaranteed to have the phrase 'good communication skills' written somewhere in the document. It is a term so overused that it is difficult to really understand what it means. In terms of employment, good communication skills are perhaps the most basic set of skills you can possess. For one to be a great communicator and have the ability to apply strong communication skills, one would need to be diverse and flexible in how they relate with others. Good communication is more or less about understanding information, asking the right questions, acquiring new skills and relaying information with ease.

In reflection of our day to day lives, even though we may be blessed with great communication skills, we still find that there is no specific or set way to communicate with other people. There are so many ways in which we try to connect and speak with loved ones, colleagues and even other species. What I have found is that the more we communicate with others, the better we become at doing so and the more we start to understand the person we are speaking to. For example, I have some friends who solely love to text, in fact I am convinced they have special powers when it comes to texting, because they text so quickly, barely looking at their phone whilst doing so. Since I got to know them, I realised that they dislike talking on the phone for a long time; however, they could send you twenty messages at a stretch. Now I still stand by the fact that it could all have been said in a five-minute conversation over the phone but that's just me, but to my 'Texter' friends, this is their preferred method of communication. Over time the closeness and mutual respect in these relationships, has enabled us to compromise by texting sometimes, and talking other times. As a result, we are able to express ourselves and communicate with each other better. I see this across most relationships; even in different cultures, the more intimate you become with others, the more you seek to communicate with them in the best possible way. Now, if we can apply this understanding to our fellow human beings, then how much more for our Heavenly Father?

There is such a variance in communication styles and how we relate with one another, that I think it's strange that when it comes to God, we believe it must be a specific or rigid way. We must understand that prayer does not just consist of repeating eloquently scripted words, nor is it limited to a specific posture or positioning of the body. Jesus specifically told us not to pray in this way, in Matthew 6:7-8, *"When you pray, don't babble on and on as people of other religions do. They think prayers are answered only by repeating words over and over again. Don't be like them, because your*

Father knows exactly what you need even before you ask him!" God wants us to be specific about our prayers. Remember, God knows what you need the most and he knows what is best for you. Ask Him what you want, in fact explain to Him why you want it, the more you begin to open up to God as I've discovered, the more you begin to see the differences between what you want and what you need.

I personally believe that prayer is like a phone call. It is essentially our direct line to God; it is a means of communication between the Creator and the creation, the establishment of a relationship between Father and child. God's desire is that we communicate with Him and build a strong and deep relationship. He earnestly wants us to speak to him as though we could physically see Him standing directly in front of us. The first man and woman had constant fellowship with God until it was cut short because of their sin and disobedience to Him. 'And they heard the voice of the LORD God walking in the garden in the cool of the day: and Adam and his wife hid themselves from the presence of the LORD God amongst the trees of the garden. And the LORD God called unto Adam, and said unto him, Where art thou?' In these two verses it is clear that there was and had been a mutual relationship between God and Man. It specifies that they could hear and determine God's footsteps walking through the Garden; this implies that they experienced a very deep closeness and intimacy with Him. We must remember that there were a variety of creatures roaming around in the Garden of Eden; but amongst all the noise, they could easily hear the footsteps of the Lord. Isn't that beautiful? Imagine that, having such a relationship with God that you can hear him walk into your room. Whilst studying this third chapter of Genesis, I discovered that this was the start of our Father's search for his lost children, his yearning to connect back and restore that love and fellowship. This is evident in His question to Adam, even though God is both omniscient and omnipresent; he still asked 'Where are you?' Dear reader, this is what God is asking you today. My beloved, where are you? I have not heard from you. Why are you hiding from me? God will never deter us from speaking to Him because **Prayer is our hearts expressed to the one who loves it best.**

One thing that we fail to understand is that God himself is a master communicator; this is evident right from the beginning when God himself spoke into the dark and formless void and called unseen things to be seen. In Genesis 1:1-26 we see God communicate what He wants to see and what He wants to happen at each stage of the creation process. Every time he wanted to do something, he spoke out and professed His desire which manifested into the heavens and earth we see and experience today. I often wonder to myself why God did not proceed to carry out what he wanted in another way; He could have just clicked his fingers. In fact he didn't have to say anything at all; He could have simply imagined the world into existence. The bible could have written something like this, Genesis 1 - 'And God went about creating the world. Six days after the world was created.' Instead the bible emphasises on every word that was spoken out by God. Why? Because there is power in our words; especially in the words we say. We must be conscious of this because it makes all the difference, in Proverbs 18:2 it says 'that the power of life and death lies in the tongue' God himself displays through the scriptures the power of speaking out and communicating, calling forth those things that are not as if they are, and as it is recorded in the bible, those things came to be.

John 1:1 says that 'In the beginning was the Word, and the Word was with God, and the Word was God.' The Passion Translation interprets the word to be 'a living expression'. This means that you have the living expression dwelling inside of you. Therefore, when you speak and declare the Word it must produce fruit, because of its inherent power... Jesus spoke of the life-giving nature of His words: "The words I have spoken to you, they are full of the Spirit and life." (John 6:63) We see the living Word of God in action every time a sinner repents and turns to Christ for eternal life. The believer's changed life bears testimony to the living, active power of the Bible. The living Word is active in the lives of those who receive it.

Since I have been walking closely with God, I have come to understand that He likes to communicate with us in diverse ways. He speaks to each of his children differently; however, even though he may communicate differently to every individual, what does not change is what He says.

"Whatever God says will NEVER be contrary to His word or lead you into sin"

If you are ever in doubt about what God is saying, always question, does this align with the word of God? Do I have an unusual peace about it? I say unusual peace because sometimes the answer may seem far-fetched, for example, God could tell someone who has never even been outside their little village and has no viable source of funding to leave their homeland and travel all the way to Fiji for a specific purpose. Now, ordinarily, this seems like a crazy and scary idea, but somewhere in that decision there will be a peace or conviction that yes, this is where I should go. In addition, God always makes provision for what you need, which is another test of whether the dialogue you are having is genuinely from God. Hearing that you need to steal, manipulate or defraud someone to get provision and money to travel to Fiji would not be God as He is not the author of confusion. Thus, ensure that when you do pray you listen out not only for what is being said, but who is saying it.

Two Way Thing

For many of us, our prayers end up looking like shopping lists and some resemble very polite, nicely written sparkly decorated Christmas letters addressed to Santa, asking him to give us our Christmas wish list for being a good boy or girl throughout the year. We end up offering our prayers to God which go something like this -

"Dear God, Thank you, (for those who even remember to say thanks). I need… I want… Please give me... provide... protect... grant me victory... grant me favour… give me joy… give me peace. As I was writing this prayer list out, God told me to interject here and tell you that some of these things which you keep praying for, you already have! You just need to read His word and walk in it; peace has already been given to you. In John 14:27, it states *"Peace I leave with you; my peace I give you. I do not give to you as the world gives. Do not let your hearts be troubled and do not be afraid."* Jesus Christ has spoken to you and affirmed that He has left you with a peace that is insurmountable because it is not of this world. Some of you reading this book are going through a situation that is troubling your mind and spirit; you may be passing through the thick of the storm right now. But God told me to tell you that He has given you the peace that surpasses all things; I dare you to simply reach out and walk in it.

Now, for the most part, we throw demands of what we want and how we want it and I guess for those who are 'really advanced' a couple of demons that need tackling down, may be added for good measure. These quick-fire round prayers sometimes may last from about three to five minutes, if that, in between scrolling through Instagram, news feeds and replying our 20+ WhatsApp messages. Being 'too busy' to speak and hear from the One who wishes to converse with us the most has become far too easy an excuse. To top it all, rather than waiting to see what God's reply to our prayer list is, we conclude our requests with a big hearty amen and go on our merry way.

This reminds me of certain types of people and the kind of conversations you tend to have with them. Just take a few seconds to think about it. Have you ever been in those types of friendships that are simply draining? The conversations that transpire are typically one sided; this is where the other person does all the talking, they never ask you about how you are or what you're doing; they just constantly talk about themselves. When you try to give an input or express your opinion, it is shut down and usually overlooked. In fact, you seldom can get a word in because they don't give you any time to respond or the opportunity to change the course of conversation. Let's be honest, when we speak to such people we are either stunned to silence, or we just avoid speaking to them altogether; we would probably see them as conceited and self-absorbed. Unfortunately, many of us are like this with God;

we call Him, He answers our call and then He hears "Hey Father!" God says: "Hello, my beloved child!" Then without second thought we talk non-stop and at the end we say "okay... yep... that's all!" I'm late for something, got to go now, bye!" And that right there is the end of the prayer and if we are honest with ourselves, this is probably the only conversation we get to have with God for the entire day.

"A lot of us speak at God rather than with Him"

Prayer is not just talking to God; it is talking with God. It involves proper dialogue and two people being patient with each other and allowing the other person to say something! Wait for God to speak. When we are praying to God we must ask ourselves is this a monologue or dialogue? Can you really call it a conversation if only one person is talking? When we have great conversations with others there is both talking and listening from both parties. There is synergy and cooperation which leads to good engagement and responsiveness. The sad part is some of us consistently talk at God, we schedule prayer times and faithfully adhere to it but in all that time, we are just constantly talking without listening. There is no effectiveness in our prayer, because we have not established a dual connection. God can and will say something back to you and give you some ideas if you let Him. It is possible that God will remind you of a verse from the Scripture that contains the answer to your query.

In my prayer time, I share my heart to God, it is such a beautiful and intimate moment, sometimes I talk to Him and even laugh with Him. Sometimes it is a word of praise or thanks, other times it is a request or a question, frustration or even an array of ideas. But I love that Jesus gives me room to speak to Him. It took me a long while but as I began to get deeper in my prayer journey, I began to pause more and give Him room to speak back to me. I listen to Him when I read the scriptures, sometimes I wait after every verse as He drops an even deeper understanding of what I'm reading into my spirit. Other times I wait on Him, even if I am writing in my own prayer journal, because He also likes to add one or two things of His own. I have learned and I am still learning to be attentive to the voice of my Father. Admittedly, this was very difficult for me to grasp at first. I did not understand that God wanted to be a part of the conversation I was having with myself, and sometimes even now I still remind myself to pause and listen. For our prayers to be effective, we must give time to God and be patient as we wait for his response to our prayers.

God Answers

Why wouldn't God want to speak to you? God spoke over the course of six days and everything He articulated came into existence. Now imagine that very same power speaking into your prayer life. Imagine the possibilities. When you pray, learn to be silent and listen, say the same thing Samuel said to God, "Speak, Lord, your servant is listening". 1 Samuel 3:1-10. This simple phrase can be the start of an extraordinary prayer life and encounter with God. As highlighted before in the previous chapter, prayer is supposed to be a two-way communication between ourselves and God. Yet many times, we don't really give Him the time to answer and listen to what He has to say. God wants us to reach out to him, and anticipate a response. In Jeremiah 33:3, He expressly says to us, "Call to me and I will answer you and I will tell you great and hidden things that you have not known." The scripture says, "I WILL ANSWER YOU." This is the part that I believe a lot of us neglect; God is telling us what he does and what his reaction will be, when we call out to him in the place of prayer, so why don't we give him the chance to answer?

My first encounter with God speaking to me taught me that not only does God hear us but He also responds. In fact I was astounded that God can actually respond to prayers with words. What I cherish most about that encounter is that I realised He deeply cared for me, not only did he care for me at that precise moment, but he always did and always will.

The night I heard his voice for the first time, I was bewildered, straddled with fear and anxiety as the cloud of depression loomed over me with every waking moment. I don't think I've ever felt so alone and afraid, it's not like I hadn't been praying before, but this time instead of praying for all these feelings to disappear, I simply confessed that I needed His help. I cried out "Speak, O Lord, I am here, and I am listening." In that moment, I managed to push aside the feelings and thoughts of fear and anxiety and listen out for what God has for me. I asked God to please speak to me clearly, I fell silent and I pressed into Him, with tears streaming down my face. Alone, huddled on the bedroom floor with only half of my duvet covers draped around me. I just lay there listening, overcome with the desire to hear the voice of God through my distress and above anything else; I knew within me that I was determined to lay there for as long as it took, until I heard Him speak. Then there it was; the warmth swathed my body like a big bear hug and I heard the voice of God; a still small voice. It was like a whisper; the most assuring, gentle, sweet tender loving voice you've ever heard. In that moment, He re-affirmed that He would 'always be with me even till the end of the world'. One of the most profound and beautiful encounters I have had with my Lord Jesus Christ. Since then, I've found myself amazed by what God chooses to reveal to me. I learned that prayer is a conversation with God and each conversation is different and unique to the individual.

"He may not encounter us in the same way, but he certainly wants to encounter us all"

Prior to my personal encounter, I believed that only the archbishops, prophets and anointed men and women of God, were the only ones who could hear the audible voice of God, let alone this young, anxious and troubled woman struggling to find herself in God. I thought to myself how can God hear me, let alone speak to me? What I forgot, is that God is known as Jehovah Shammah; God is always there for us. We just need to be patient in our hearts and mind and trust that He will communicate with us whenever we call upon him. Our Father in Heaven really looks forward to those moments when we take the time out in our day to spend with Him. God has so many things He wants to say to us. Most of the time we miss out on the revelations that God has for us, because we're so quick to get to the closing chapter of the book, we do not take time to start from the beginning and enjoy the full story.

Many times, we pray out of desperation or an anguishing desire to be delivered and set free from whatever troubles our hearts. Other times we only resort to prayer because we want something from God, a quick fix and easy solution. In doing so, we miss the deeper relationship and intimate experience we can have with God. We treat God as if He were a genie promising to grant our wishes. Remember, prayer is a two-way street. God wants us to come to Him with our requests and desires but God wants to say something too and we must be ready to receive what He has to say. Until I changed my approach to prayer and prayed to listen, not just to be heard, I had been accustomed to just sending up those quick-fire round prayers along with the occasional please and thank you's. I hadn't kept my eyes and ears open for a response. But when I did, this changed my entire prayer life. Sometimes I wait a long time until I hear His voice, sometimes I wait and I don't hear anything at all and that's okay, there are times where we need to learn to just "wait on the Lord." He doesn't have to speak if He doesn't want to or need to. If you don't hear anything on the first day, do it again the next day and the next after that. If it takes a week, do it for a week. Do it for as long as it takes until you hear God speaking to you. The main thing is to give God time. Tell Him, **"Father, this is your time. Speak to me! I am listening**". **God will talk to you**" because He has promised that.

I often hear people ask, "Well how do you hear the voice of God?" I see this question come up time and time again; there are many publications, sermons and broadcasts on this topic explaining and training people to hear the voice of God, whilst I do not dispute the necessity to be enlightened in this area. I think the actual question should be, how to listen to what God says when He speaks? Often God has already spoken; we are the ones not listening to what He is saying. Sometimes we are trying to get a different answer from what we know in our hearts is the true answer. At times it can be difficult to accept, even heart-breaking, especially when it is relative to other human relationships or things we believe we have a right to hold on to. This reminds me of the anguish Jesus Christ felt in the garden of Gethsemane, when He knew the Will of the Father was for him to endure the cross and die for the sins of the World, but I suppose momentarily He struggled with this plan and sought an alternative answer. However, within the midst of this inner struggle, Jesus turned it into a prayer which resulted in Him concluding and gathering the strength to both accept and carry out the will of God.

This is why, prayer is fundamental for a Christian believer, we pray essentially to know and carry out the will of God for our lives. It is not what I tell God that it is the most important thing in prayer; it is what God wants to tell me. Is there anything you can tell Him that He does not already know? Is there anything at all? You may think that no one knows what you are going through, no one knows the problems you have or how hard your life is. Now, this may apply to other people but not to God. God knows everything! Even before you start praying, God knows everything you want to tell Him and why these things are happening. Moreover, he knows the way out of your situation. So, if you just come to God say what you want and leave, you wouldn't really be able to say anything different to what he already knows. On the other hand, He can tell you many things you do not know. He has so many things to reveal to you so that you learn the reasons of your problems or needs. He can give you the wisdom you need, if only you would listen and wait for His answer.

How Should We Pray?

People often question prayer because they have a desire to pray but they don't really know how to. The problems is that, sometimes we over complicate prayer and make it a mystical and magical thing, while we cannot negate the power and supernatural abilities of prayer, it is really simple. Speak. Believe God is there, and that He will hear and answer your prayers. Sometimes prayer is treated like a prescribed formula. The belief is that, if you do not execute these specific methods, techniques, timings and prescriptions, it will not work! There are people out there today who think if they do not kneel with heads bowed or lay prostrate before an altar or inside a church, God will not be able to hear their prayers. This is so far removed from the truth; we should look at prayer as a maths equation. There are many different methods to solving an equation. If those methods are done correctly, they will always lead to the correct answer. In the same light, a response to your prayer is not dependent on whether you knelt-down or stood up, whether you prayed in English or Aramaic. It is about the condition of your heart towards God and your belief in Him.

"God is after what is in your heart, Your relationship with him is what matters"

1 John 5:14-15 says that we should come to God with our prayers, with the assurance that He hears and will grant us such requests if it is in alignment with His will. Praying according to the will of God is a general pattern we see across the bible. It illustrates that God will answer our prayers if what we are praying for is in accordance to his will and would bring glory and honour back to His name.

Jesus Christ lays out a model answer to his disciples of how we ought to pray in Matthew 6:9-13. (The Lord's Prayer)

Our Father who is in heaven; this acknowledges and addresses God as the one you are speaking to.

Hallowed be your name; we should give adoration with emphasis on honour to God and His name.

Your kingdom come; we are to pray for God's kingdom which is to pray for the people of God, this is a Spiritual request to save the lost, to bring God's divine wisdom and His peace within his church.

Your will be done; we are to pray that God's desires are fulfilled here on earth and acknowledge him as sovereign.

Give us this day our daily bread; we are to pray for our daily provisions, material requests; food, job, health and day-to-day provisions.

Forgive us our debts as we forgive others; we are to pray and confess our sins and request for forgiveness as well as placing those who have wronged us into God's hands and forgiving them.

Lead not into temptation, deliver from evil; we are to pray and ask God to keep us from falling into temptation and God's protective power and deliverance from Satan and his powers.

Yours is the kingdom, the power and glory; we are to give adoration to God and referencing him as the one who owns all.

Amen; Close of prayer: Literally, "so be it".

Jesus gives us a pattern for how we should pray and the kind of things that should be included in the prayers we offer to God. This model highlights some of the key areas we should focus on in our prayer lives. This is not to be misunderstood as a set way to pray, nor is it a mere recital. We need to cram in our minds and continually repeat back to God. Jesus was trying to make the disciples aware that to pray is much more than just repetition of words. Our prayers should include praises and thanksgiving to God. We should admit our faults, we should cast our worries of what we will eat and what we will do unto Him, trusting him to provide and take care of our needs, having done all that, submit to His will and great plan for our lives and for those around us.

Moreover, before Jesus goes ahead to tell the disciples how they should be praying, he first states how not to pray and the type of things that do not result in answered prayers. He explains this in Matthew 6:5-7 *"And now about prayer. When you pray, don't be like the hypocrites who love to pray publicly on street corners and in the synagogues where everyone can see them. I assure you that is all the reward they will ever get. But when you pray, go away by yourself, shut the door behind you, and pray to your Father secretly. Then your Father, who knows all secrets, will reward you."* These are the issues that some of us are having with prayer. In verse 5, Christ details to us that our prayer should not be done in a way that primarily showcases our sole purpose to be seen and heard or for us to be considered more righteous or holier than others. This point is important because it is re-emphasized by Jesus in (Luke 18:9-10). *"Then Jesus told this story to some who had great confidence in their own righteousness and scorned everyone else: "Two men went to the Temple to pray. One was a Pharisee, and the other was a despised tax collector." The Pharisee stood by himself and prayed this prayer: 'I thank you, God, that I am not a sinner like everyone else. For I don't cheat, I don't sin, and I don't commit adultery. I'm certainly not like that tax collector! I fast twice a week, and I give you a tenth of my income.'*

This Pharisee's prayer sounds a lot like some of our own personal prayers to God. We may not say the exact same words but by praying in such manner, we are trying to show others that we are holier, In essence we saying we are entitled to God's blessings because we have kept a few of His commandments. We believe that we have acquired righteousness in our own strength and works but God himself said in his word that our righteousness is like a filthy rag before him. This prayer is self-seeking and self-gratifying, not once is God brought into the prayer aside to call His attention to our long list of what we have accomplished.

"But the tax collector stood at a distance and dared not even lift his eyes to heaven as he prayed. Instead, he beat his chest in sorrow, saying, 'O God, be merciful to me, for I am a sinner.' I tell you, this sinner, not the Pharisee, returned home justified before God. For those who exalt they will be humbled, and those who humble themselves will be exalted." (Luke 18:11-14)

Pharisees were the respected holy men of those days whereas tax collectors were often treated as the bad guys, by mere appearance alone one would assume that Jesus would rebuke the tax collector. Thanks be to God that our prayers are not based on what we look like or the kind of jobs we do or how many times we attend church in the year. The Pharisee attempts to validate his own "righteousness" through his prayer. He is full of pride while spurting out his good deeds. The tax collector approaches his prayer in humility and no self-righteousness. He asks God to show him mercy. What God is trying to show us in this parable is that our attitude and the motive of our hearts is important as we come to God in prayer. The question we must ask ourselves is. Have I come before God as a tax collector or as a Pharisee?

When we pray, we should always check our intent. Does the prayer honour God and exalt His name? What is the purpose behind the prayer? Do you pray for others to be blessed and encouraged? Are your prayers done in humility? Are your prayers focused on obtaining godly wisdom, counsel and direction because God is pleased with such prayers and answers them. Using the Lord's Prayer as a guideline, we can use our own words, relationship, revelation and experience to communicate with our Father. Freely expressing our hearts to Him without restraint of which posture or which way to face or not face. It should be a real personal conversation between a Father and his child. If the child knows the Father well, such child will know how to speak to their Father and will be able to hear and discern His voice. I have no doubt in my heart and mind that God has so many things he wants to tell you and speak to you about. He is simply waiting for you to start the conversation.

"Believe He is there and listening, because He is. Believe He will help you, because He will"

In summary, here are four simple steps to get you started and restarted again in this new exciting and adventurous prayer journey. Although, I relay a few prayer points and guidelines throughout this book, it is much more important to open your heart and mind to God. **Use these practical steps to start until you become comfortable** and familiar enough in speaking with Him and from there you can create your own steps, pattern and style of communication to Him.

Create Time

Before you begin, try and schedule a time, almost like an appointment, not to be drastic, instead try to train your mind to think of it as a doctor's appointment or a very important business meeting. You can set an alarm, reminders, write it down or simply prepare your mind that at this time, I would like to start this conversation with God. God really honours the appointments we make with Him. So once you have made a promise to meet with Him, please make sure you do. You don't want to be the one who stood God up.

Relax and Start

The next step is to find a quiet place where you feel comfortable, relaxed and have no distractions. This can be anywhere, from the living room, to a silent study, a nearby park or a garden. Once you have found a convenient place, from there you can begin to talk to him. A good way to address him would be by His name, you can say "Dear God" or "Heavenly Father," "Our Father which art in heaven," or simply "God." As you begin to form a habit of quiet time with Him, you will begin to encounter him in different ways and get a deeper revelation of who He is. From my experience, as I have spent time with him, sometimes I call him "Yahweh", "Almighty God", "Daddy" and I am still learning different facets of Him with each given day.

Open up

Now that you have begun, just continue and speak from your heart and share your dreams and desires as well as your worries and problems. Be real, tell him about the person who upset you or caused you pain, and the people you might have caused pain too. You can ask Him for comfort, direction, understanding, or healing. Whatever is on your mind, bring it to Him, acknowledging that His wisdom and timing are greater than yours. You can ask Him what He wants for you. Your prayer can also be about those around you, your family and friends, you can pray for their needs and desires too or ask for ways you can help and show love to them.

Give thanks

Lastly, in all that you say, do not forget to give thanks to God. This can be at the start, middle or end of your prayer. Express appreciation to God for all the blessings in your life. Remember, even challenges can be a blessing, although at the time of the challenge it rarely ever looks like it. Trust me, I can attest to that fact, but God uses this to bring out the humility in us, which keeps our hearts and minds open to God's answers.

End your prayer

Once you've said all that you wanted to say, you can end your prayer by saying, "In Jesus name I pray, amen." This is not in any way a setting stone or a must but I put this to you as a final step. Jesus is the way to connect to our Father in Heaven and all things should be done in His name, the final part of the prayer is to say "Amen" at the end. Amen simply means 'so be it'. This is to show that we are in intentional about what we are praying about and we believe that in accordance with God's will those things shall come to be.

CHAPTER 1 PRAYER POINTS

1. Dear Father, teach me how to have a two-way conversation with you, with you more effectively

2. Dear Father, draw me closer to You, close enough for me to hear Your footsteps Lord

3. Dear Father, train my ears to clearly hear your voice, when you speak to me

4. Dear Father, give me the grace to pray with patience and wait to hear what you have to say

5. Dear Father, please give me the grace to obey your instructions when you speak to me

6. Dear Father, help me to manage my time effectively so that I can spend more time with you in the place of prayer

7. Dear Father, Your word say when I call upon you, you will answer, please answer my requests today

God communicates with us through the Holy Spirit, in the form of good thoughts, ideas, strong peaceful feelings and sometimes convicting truths. When we feel those things, it means God is encouraging us, showing us truth, and giving us direction. He creates an avenue to which we come to the realisation of how incredibly wonderful we are in His eyes. The Holy Spirit supports and helps us take charge of our entire lives. This helps us to discover our God-given talents, inner wisdom and strength.

Interestingly, we must understand that everyone will feel and respond to the Holy Spirit differently. Over the years, I have come to realise that the Holy Spirit is a personable spirit. He moves within the individual, the way he wants to, depending on the relationship, understanding, intimacy and responsiveness of the individual, that's why encountering the Holy Spirit, differs from person to person. In the Bible, the spirit of God is sometimes described as a "still small voice," (1 Kings 19:11–12). In my own case I can only describe it as; "it seems like God is whispering to your mind".

In the book of Acts, the encounter the apostles had with the Holy Spirit was described as a mighty rushing wind which resulted in their speech being likened to tongues of fire. I marvel at the thought of what that might have looked like. The witnesses around the apostles at that time accused them of all being drunk; that is to show you that what might look strange to you or peculiar, can actually be from God. This is not to say that all things that look different must be from God. It is just worthy to note that it is not always what is within our own ideology of norm that sets precedent for what is of God. But if you continue to partner with the Holy Spirit, He will teach you discernment and further renew your mind to see things from His perspective which is the supernatural over the natural.

The Holy Spirit helps us to pray by giving us revelation of God's word. Often, we "do not know what to pray for" (Romans 8:26). The Holy Spirit helps aligns our prayers with the will of the Father, He converts and directs our prayers into what we ought to be praying for, how we are to pray, who we are to pray for and at times, when and where we ought to pray. The Holy Spirit is essential to praying effectually; praying without the Holy Spirit to me is like shooting arrows without having a target. It is aimless and has no purpose. The Holy Spirit is a beautiful and powerful part of who God is. Through His power, we have a great aid in our prayer lives and a conduit to become who God created us to be.

He Intercedes.

I don't know if you can relate, but sometimes I really have no words to express my feelings and other times I have so much to say that I'm not sure where to start. This is where the Holy Spirit comes to let you know exactly what to say. In Romans 8:26 it says: *"Likewise the Spirit helps us in our weakness. For we do not know what to pray for as we ought, but the Spirit himself intercedes for us with groanings too deep for words"*. The Holy Spirit is such a compassionate helper that he comes to us 'in our weaknesses". When I meditated on this verse I understood that sometimes it is in our messy, broken and dejected state that the Holy Spirit comes to our assistance. One of the biggest misconceptions of prayer and praying to God is that we must be well put together to do so. This couldn't be further from the truth. God doesn't want our cover ups, pretentious smiles and hollow 'I'm fine' speech. He just wants us to be real with Him. When I look at the life of King David, I understand why God said of Him that he was a man after his Heart'. He was someone that was completely vulnerable before God. He never tried to hide his flaws and even though he was King over the whole of Israel, he never acted as if he had it all together before God.

In the same way, the Holy Spirit wants us to be vulnerable with Him, to pour into him, to trust him with our requests; desires, hopes, needs and trust that He has the best plan for our lives. Prayer is a form of surrender. We pray to God because we believe in His ability to answer us in the best possible way and to carry out His perfect will for our lives. The Holy Spirit helps our weaknesses by interceding and praying for us. The intercessory work of Christ is invaluable to every Christian, this intercession can be summarised in Hebrews 4:13, which states that we are to *"draw near to God through him"*, we are able to come to God through the cause of Christ. Who better to go through than the one who was born into sin and conquered it? The beauty of this is that when we are praying, Jesus understands our weaknesses and the Holy Spirit, through that understanding, helps us in those weaknesses. He prays for us and his prayers are answered, because he prays perfectly based on his perfect sacrifice. This truth is prevalent even when our minds try to tell us otherwise, this means that even though we may hear voices telling us that we are not good enough to be forgiven, our sin is too much or too big. Remember that the sacrifice of Christ is constantly defending speaking and interceding for us in direct opposition to such thoughts. Our ongoing salvation before God is cemented through the finished work of the cross; the death and resurrection of Jesus Christ. We talk about salvation as a thing of the past; that one-time event where we decided to accept him and then that was it. Understand that even today we are being saved by the propitiation of Christ and therefore just as **Jesus is interceding for us in heaven to maintain our redemption, the Holy Spirit intercedes for us on earth to make our prayers acceptable according to that redemption.**

He Burdens Us

The Holy Spirit reveals things we do not know and does so in accordance with the will of God. One of the ways the Holy Spirit helps us in prayer is by giving us a strong urge or desire to pray. That desire can lead you to pray for a specific thing or person, this feeling has often been referred to as a prayer burden. This is not always specified in the time of prayer, it could just be a desire to pray a general prayer and dwell in God's presence, or to offer prayers of adoration and thanksgiving to Him.

I love the words of one of God's General and a prominent writer on the subject of prayer, Edward M. Bounds. He states that *"The habit of praying is a good habit and should be early and strongly formed; but to pray by habit merely is to destroy the life of prayer and allow it to degenerate into a hollow and sham-producing form. Habit may form the bank for the river of prayer, but there must be a strong, deep, pure current, crystal and life-giving, flowing between these two banks."* That strong, deep, pure current, crystal and life-giving river I believe is the Holy Spirit. He puts meaning and vitality into our prayers so that we are not just praying out of customary traditions and routines, but rather, out of a God given desire. As we allow the Spirit of God to fill our hearts and minds, He transfers God's burden to us, He draws us deep into the soul of God. It is in this state that we can see and discern the will of God.

The Spirit of God may also share with us the desperate needs of the nations and individual people. The spirit of God places the desire and heart of God within us, so in our personal time of prayer we begin to plead and intercede for others with a weighty understanding of God's love for them. When it comes to prayer, without the Holy Spirit we will be lost. Without His Spirit, you will find that naturally you have no real desire to pray, but thanks be to God that the Holy Spirit is always willing to help us pray. He does this by putting a burden on our heart to show us what or who to pray for. He also shows and reveals to us many things about prayer, this can occur whilst we are still praying or before we even start.

He Guides Us in Prayer

The Holy Spirit can teach us how to listen out for Him, by revealing himself to us in diverse ways. He sometimes does this through His word, circumstances or uses the people who are close to us and at times even distant strangers. At times the Holy Spirit can begin to unfold the value of certain scriptures and explain them so that as you pray, you draw strength from the word of the Lord and use it to support your prayer points. I personally have been in the place of prayer and the spirit of the Lord begins to drop scriptures in my spirit and sometimes I have never come across them or read them before. This is the Holy Spirit guiding my prayers and aligning my prayer patterns with the will of God. He is such a great teacher that he gives us direction about how to approach God in prayer, which may be that He brings to our remembrance some of the promises of God spoken over us or through scriptures, to give you a basis for your prayers. At times the spirit of God can just prompt me to pray and then start to direct my prayers, which often can be different to what I originally started praying about. We may start off our prayers like this; "I want you to do this for me, in this way and at this set time, through this particular person," but at the end of the prayer we may find ourselves praying, 'I surrender all to you, my wants, my needs, have your way in my life, do what you will in my life o sovereign God'. Therefore, the power and presence of the Holy Spirit in our prayer life is invaluable, because He brings us to the place where our prayers become conformed to the image of His son.

He Helps Us to Wait Patiently

One of the biggest lessons I have learned is that effective prayers don't go well with hurry. Now, this is not to say that God cannot bring about your request speedily. In fact, on the contrary, it says in the book of Isaiah 60:22: *'A little one shall become a thousand, and a small one a strong nation: I the LORD will hasten it in his time.'* God is very instantaneous, as soon as He speaks, there is a reaction and awesomeness follows. Just like in the beginning in Genesis 1:2 when He said *"Let there be light, and there was light."* It was an immediate response. God really does want to give us our heart's desire but he also wants to ensure that we get certain things at the right time and in that process of waiting, we learn and grow. He brings out our faith and ability to trust in him more. In Romans 8:25 it says *'For in this hope we were saved. But hope that is seen is no hope at all. Who hopes for what they already have? But if we hope for what we do not yet have, we wait for it patiently'.* It continues to say that we groan within ourselves, that groaning is also a time of waiting. The Holy Spirit groans with us as He makes intercession for us and helps us to pray that we would wait patiently.

That word *'patience'*. I don't know if this is you too but I am at a constant war with patience because the truth of the matter is most times; I don't want it later; I want it now! However, in my impatience I discovered that **when things are done prematurely, it is not without consequence.** For example, my baby cousin; she is hungry, and she wishes to eat, whilst I am preparing the milk she is exercising her lung muscles and voice box in protest to me that she is in desperate need of food. To be honest, I've always wondered if this is how we sound to God as we plead, cry, wail, shout, scream our hearts desires out to Him, whilst He is busy preparing that very thing we need. As I prepare her food, and bring it near enough, her crying and wailing increases but now the food is hot. As her guardian it would be extremely foolish and cruel to put the piping hot food directly into her mouth all because she is crying and wailing. I would like to believe that you also think the same way as me. Now if you and I can come to such a conclusion, then why do you think God wouldn't show the same love and care towards us? Like my baby cousin, sometimes we tend to want things on impulse, we want things right away without realising the negative consequences we could face but just like a good parent and guardian, God can see ahead and knows what is and what is not right for us at a specific time. Being the omnipotent God that He is, He knows what we can handle and therefore we must trust his guidance and the process in which he takes us through.

Prayer and Patience, I like to call it the 2P rule. I must admit it took me a long time to fully understand this rule and I'm still working on it, however, if like me, you're able to understand this principle, it will become a great aid and help to you in the place of prayer. I wouldn't call myself the most patient person. In fact I like things done very quickly, which always leads me to look for the quickest, alternative, short-cut available. The best to tell you about prayer and patience is the way the Holy Spirit explained seeds and farming to me; the first time you pray about any situation, it is like a seed. Some seeds can be so powerful that they can start to blossom on their own without much attention, especially if the soil is very moist. For example there are certain flowers, vegetables and fruits that grow very quickly in good soil conditions. Bush-beans, celosia, marigold and cosmos sprout, these types of seeds in good soil require very little attention. These seeds can start growing and budding within three to five days.

However, most of our 'prayer seeds' as I like to call them, need more attention and care, specifically for the type of seed planted. Therefore, we need to pause and listen to the Holy Spirit because he is like the God-Father of Farmers. He knows a whole lot about farming (He did create and cater to the biggest garden in the Universe; Earth). So whilst we are praying, the Holy Spirit comes and informs us about what we need for the prayer seed to grow and blossom. This is why it is important to listen, because the more we get clear instructions, the more we learn how best to grow our 'prayer seed'. The Holy Spirit whispers, now water it, prune it, add a garden trellis to it, leave it, add garlic, pepper spray to get rid of the bugs. Therefore, the more we pray the more the seed grows until we get to the last prayer needed for that seed to fully blossom and fulfil its purpose.

What I realised from this analogy of the prayer seeds is that, when it comes to prayer, we either do one of two things and sometimes we do both. The first is that we start off with the seed, we take it in our hand and plant it and then we walk away. After some time when we remember, we come back and have a look at it, stare at it long and hard or in other cases scream, shout and cry in frustration at the seed and then proceed to walk away and then repeat the same cycle. What this means is that we start off rightly by praying then after that one time of prayer, it all stops. We do not attempt to pray about it anymore then after sometime we remember the situation again but this time instead of praying about it, we just worry about it and get frustrated with the unchanging situation (lack of growth from the seed) but instead of praying, we complain and moan about it.

The second thing we do is take the seed in our hands and then plant it, but then we proceed to manhandle the seed, because we are trying to add water when we are to let the sun access it, we are cutting too much off, pruning when we are supposed to leave it, we don't add support to the stalk, we are spraying the wrong substances on the plant which at times stunts the growth of the seed or the seed grows with deformities. What do I mean by this? Sometimes we ignore the leading of the Holy Spirit in the place of prayer. We try to grow the seed with what we feel is right, without the knowledge of the farmer. Sometimes we are praying, and we don't allow the Holy Spirit to teach us how to pray and align to the will of the father. When we don't give heed to the Holy Spirit, we end up praying ineffectively because we have our own ideology how the prayer should look and in our desire for our prayers to be answered we add what we shouldn't add and take out what should be in.

When we are waiting or trusting God for something, we must learn to lean into Him more by waiting patiently to hear his instructions. This will save us more time than when we go and start doing things by ourselves. This is why some of us are waiting unnecessarily, just take a moment and think of some of the prayers you've made before that are yet to be answered and sincerely ask yourself, why am I waiting? As I've discovered myself, we often say **we are waiting on God but sometimes God is waiting on you?**

Down below is a short summary of how you can allow the Holy Spirit to help you work in and through your prayer life.

1. Firstly, please note that you are not always expected to know the will of God every time and that's okay. This is where you exercise your faith and trust in the ability of the Holy Spirit, allowing him to express what you don't know on your behalf. Isn't that amazing that we have someone who knows the will of God when we don't? Don't carry the burden of not knowing the will of God, let the Holy Spirit do this for you.

2. Understand that in your disappointment, seasons of confusion and moments of silence that you are not being ignored, God is not hiding His face from you to tease you. God is very much amid every situation both in times of testimony and trial. God is searching your heart, and he is finding in your groaning, a deeper meaning. In your groaning **He is revealing Himself, for you to discover yourself and then moulding what you've found into the image of Christ**.

3. Even in your weakness, the spirit of God is praying for you and not against you. The spirit of God intercedes for us. His spirit is not condemning us but rather convicting our hearts to conform to the will of the Father. His spirit helps

us in times of uncertainty and pain. The spirit of God is on our side, advocating for our good.

4. Lastly, I want you to know that God, the Father hears prayers of the spirit. Those unknown tongues that you cannot always interpret, He understands that gentle humming, vehement wails and silent whimpers. It is always heard. God does not reject the prayers of God. Therefore, lean into the wisdom of the Holy Spirit and allow Him to express to the Father what needs to be said.

CHAPTER 2 PRAYER POINTS

1. Dear Father, help me to pray in accordance with your will

2. Dear Father, place the burden of prayer in my heart that I might intercede for others as well as for myself

3. Dear Father, guide my prayer, help me to water and carefully grow my prayer seeds so they can blossom

4. Dear Father, help me to wait patiently in the midst of prayer, so that I might be led by your spirit

THE POWER OF PRAYER

If there is anything I am confident about, it is the power of prayer. There really is nothing else like it. Often, I feel we underestimate the power that comes with prayer.

"Prayer is the key that we use to open the door and gain access to a whole new world of possibilities"

However, this power can only be fully realised when we uncover the depths of our relationship with God. Discovering the power of prayer allows God to express Himself through our lives. Isn't it wonderful that people get to see God's glory in us and through us? This occurs only when we put God first in our lives. However, I have found that instead of choosing God as first priority, we treat God as if he is the "backup plan". We only include him in the picture when things have spiralled out of control. This is not the kind of relationship God wants to build with us in prayer. Some of us have some regard for the power of prayer but only in a very distant way. We treat God like a distant elderly relative that we are forced to visit every now and then. We tell them a short summary of what we are up to with our lives and what we would have them do for us if possible, we may request their presence for some kind of occasion and we don't bother them until next year or until something else comes up. Such relationships are superficial, self-interested and usually riddled with guilt. There is no real relationship only obligation and duty.

"Powerful prayers flow out of a genuine relationship"

These types of prayers naturally come out as part of a bigger 'conversation'. Paul pens down the necessity of this type of conservation by stating that we should *'pray without ceasing'*. When we start to incorporate the habit of prayer into our daily lives, then we tap into an unlimited supply of benefits. Such conversations create an atmosphere where we can transcend to a different realm, closing the gap between the spiritual and physical. This type of relationship is primarily built on a foundation of trust that comes from the knowledge of God. It's the knowledge of Him that's at the heart of Christianity. It's in this relationship that we are transformed by His love and in which our lives are completely transformed. Just like our earthly relationships, it takes time to get to know someone. It's in our getting to know them that we come to know not just what they've done, but also what they will or will not do. Without relationship with God, Christianity is just another dead religion. His invitation to prayer is about love, He wants to "father" us. He wants to love and protect us. He wants to provide for us. The beautiful thing about that is prayer gives us the provision for all of this and more.

One Must Pray

One must pray! This may seem obvious, but a person cannot expect to experience the power of prayer unless they 'actually' pray. Prayer gives us direct access to the throne of Grace; to God the Father, God the Son and God the Holy Spirit. Without prayer

I honestly do not know how any Christian can survive, function or even live. When we pray we are saying that we believe that our Father in heaven will answer and bring a solution to our request.

Even Jesus, the Son of God, lived such a life of prayer that there is not one prayer in the bible that Jesus prayed that was unanswered. Every prayer that Jesus prayed was effectual, more so that even when he seemingly could not bear the task ahead, he prayed until His prayer became answerable unto God, by saying 'not my will but yours, Lord'. Jesus rarely prayed for himself. Instead he prayed for the needs of others and those of His friends. Similarly, Prophet Samuel clearly understood the importance of prayer and the importance of unselfish prayers. In (1 Samuel 12:23) he told the people: "Moreover as for me, God forbid that I should sin against the LORD in ceasing to pray for you: but I will teach you the good and the right way". Samuel's prayer was directed for the best interests of the people and not his own selfish interests. Looking at the needs of others and taking it up in prayer is far superior than praying for our own selfish desires. While I am not discrediting praying for our personal needs, we should recognise that the needs of others are just as important. Jesus throughout his life prayed for others. He also repeatedly spoke on the importance of prayer. "And he spoke a parable unto them to this end, that men ought to always pray, and not to faint" (Luke 18:1), that is, even when you want to give up, or sometimes in my own words, when I feel like 'I'm over it' Jesus is saying yes, do not stop praying.

Be Consistent

When I read through the Bible, I see so many amazing stories about the power of prayer. However, I have come to realise that we as people don't pray consistently enough to experience those amazing stories ourselves. Consistency, by dictionary definition is acting or doing something in the same way over time, especially to be fair or accurate, as well as conforming to a regular pattern or style. This definition is why I believe that consistency and prayer were made for each other. Why? Well, because more than anything, prayer allows us to communicate with God directly and when we do that consistently over time, we begin to communicate fairly and accurately with Him, conforming to His regular pattern and style.

Prayer is a bit like exercising. To maintain fitness or ascertain a certain physique, you cannot just exercise once and expect life changing results. Such results come through time and consistency; every new habit takes time to develop. The world's most famous athletes don't just become skilled overnight. Serena Williams, Cristiano Ronaldo and Lewis Hamilton are not overnight successes; they have achieved all that they have because of consistent practice. To be the best talent, one must consistently become better; this applies to all of us, no matter what we do. The more consistently we practice at our interests and our jobs, the better we are at them. The great people we talk about, stalk their Instagram pages and search for on Wikipedia didn't just sit around waiting for their gifts to just evolve, rather they composed, trained, revised and edited whether they felt like it or not until the work was finished. This same approach is essential to the effectiveness of our prayer lives.

Prayer is a key part of God's plan to release forerunners across the world, to demonstrate His power and glory whilst preparing the way for Jesus's return. In an hour of increasing darkness, the

Lord is calling believers to behold Him, become who He made them to be, and boldly declare that to others. Consistent prayer helps us to understand this better and realise that we are his children living in unity with Him and experiencing heaven on earth. Once we have this constant communion with Him, we will see that answered prayers are a daily experience. There is nothing that prayer cannot change or heal, including disease, hurt, pain and loss. Prayer reforms human thought and experience through spiritual power. The more consistent we are about praying, the more we feel the great effects of our prayers.

Be Persistent

If you are searching for a deeper understanding of God, you'll find that prayer helps. The more persistent you are in the place of prayer, the more you are enabled to handle the peaks and troughs of life. When we determine to make praying a consistent and permanent part of our daily experience, we will inevitably improve our lives. That is not to say that because we pray constantly our lives will be without challenges. Sin, disappointment, lack, and trials cross our paths daily, in various ways. Just like Christ said *'these things I have spoken to you, that in me you may have peace. In the world you shall have distress: but have confidence, I have overcome the world'.* Likewise, Jesus has overcome, by showing us how to consistently be in communion with the Father. Our persistent prayer keeps us from accepting anything evil as ordained by God and helps us eliminate those thoughts from our minds by 'casting down evil imaginations which try to acknowledge itself above the knowledge of God'. When faced with obstacles or suffering, we can, through prayer say, "*I foreseaw the Lord, always before my face, for he is on my right hand, that I should not be moved*" (Acts 2:25). God is always 'before our face'. We cannot stop our God-given right to bare our face before Him. By praying persistently, we'll find that we too, will overcome and accomplish great things. Once we utilise the privilege of praying before God, we'll find that God is the true absolute power and evil has no power over us at all.

Persistent prayer is that kind of prayer where you don't give up, even when you can't see any results. It may have been weeks, months or even years, but you continue to pray anyway. As we have explored above, the word consistent means doing something the same way over time; whereas persistent means continuing to do something despite all the challenges and difficulties. This is the main difference between consistent and persistent. These traits can be found in the bible by two great women of God, who applied these principles along with unwavering faith through effectual prayers which led to availing results.

Hannah

Hannah was a childless woman who suffered much, but she took refuge in God. Her husband had taken a second wife, Peninnah, who bore him children and as a result, taunted Hannah because she could not. Hannah's husband offered his love and gifts, wanting to reassure Hannah of his love towards her. But Hannah still desired to have her own child and become a mother. Every person, at one point in life, experiences a desire that will not be quenched by material things and circumstances that causes grief, even when their loved ones are around. Every year, Hannah would go to worship and participate in the church ceremonies, despite the pain she felt, she still offered sacrifices, thanksgiving, praise and prayers to God. She continued to "show up! Now when you pray, do you just pray a few times and when the answer doesn't come, you just give up and then go on about your daily life? Hannah entered Shiloh broken, unhappy and defeated. Her mind and her heart lost in the rejection and shame brought on by her barrenness. However, one particular year, Hannah decided to focus on God and His provision instead of dwelling on her unchanging circumstances. Instead of standing in the outer courts, Hannah did something that brought her into the inner court of God's presence; she cried a wordless prayer of deep groaning, cutting through the deep disappointment of her barrenness; these prayers, carried from the heart, proceeded to change nations.

My question to you is; when was the last time you took your pain in prayer to the Lord? Are you prone to run away and stop praying because you have experienced disappointment? Or have you in your pain, run to the Lord with transparency, telling him the truth, 'God, I'm really hurting and I'm in pain here, help me"? The prayers that God answers are real prayers from the heart, regardless of time, place or technique. Hannah's story gives us insight into God's heart. God does not despise human desires. Many times, we simply do not understand these things. In the life of Hannah, we see that God knows our story from the very beginning and that everything has a purpose. Hannah's longing for a child was not a desire that God was shunning away or discrediting. God did not chastise her for being discontent. We know that godly contentment is great gain but that does not mean that our human desires, even those that overwhelm us with sorrow, when they are unmet, are sinful in God's eyes. He understands our feelings. He knows that *a hope deferred makes the heart sick*" (Proverbs 13:12). Here Hannah was at the lowest point in her life, offering up a request that she had probably spoken about a thousand times. Having been beaten down and disappointed, do you find it hard to ask God for something boldly and specifically in prayer? I know I do. The Bible says we don't receive, because we don't ask. Don't give up on asking for what you most desire. If it is healing, ask, if it's a spouse, ask and if it's a child, ask him but do it believing that God gives good gifts to those who ask, because He is a rewarder of all those who seek Him.

Though Hannah didn't know when she would conceive, she prayed having faith, without any doubts, even though she couldn't see the answers, she was confident that God cared. After her prayer, she reacted as if she already received the answer. God healed not just her physical body so that she could bear children, but God also restored her spirit through her renewed faith and emotional state by giving her gladness. In 1 Samuel 1:18 It is recorded that Hannah began to eat again, (previously she had stopped eating because of this sorrow and discontent) and she was no longer sad. God is concerned with your whole entire being: body, mind, spirit and soul. His desire is beyond just giving you what you need, He wants to make you whole.

After years of praying for the same thing, most of us would eventually have given up. Hannah did not. She was devout and relentless in her request to God, until he finally answered her prayers. Hannah teaches us to never give up, to honour our promises to God, and to praise God for his wisdom and kindness. Hannah persevered, even though God was silent toward her request for a child for many years, she never stopped praying. Hannah was mocked by Peninnah and rebuked by Eli, but heard by God. As a result of Hannah's persistent prayers, she got more than she could have ever expected. Her son became a priest before God, a judge of Israel, a mighty prophet, the establisher of the kings of Israel, and an instrument in bringing the nation back to God. She bore seven children.

"Let's all pray as Hannah did, consistently and persistently, and with full faith in God"

Jochebed

This reminds me of another persistent believer in the bible, Jochebed. She believed her child would be great. You might say well every mother thinks that about their child. The difference is, Jochebed followed up her belief with action, and she just knew from birth that there was something uniquely different about this particular child. At this time, the child had been born into a dark and apocalyptic era, in which Pharaoh had passed a barbarous decree that all Hebrew male children should be slain. Despite this frightening reality, Jochebed believed and trusted God for the safe keeping of her child during such perilous times. She decided that she was not going to succumb to the decrees of the evil doers; but instead she put her utmost faith in God, and in doing so God gave her the wisdom to be able to protect her baby from the hands of Pharaoh. God gave her such a boldness and wisdom that after the baby was a few months old, she was able to build a mini basket boat and set her son upon the river, trusting God that His eye will watch over her small baby boy in this makeshift boat. As we read on in the story, God responded by sending the Pharaoh's daughter to find the basket. What really amazes me is that the daughter of Pharaoh (the man who made the decree) was the one who ended up looking after Moses, the Hebrew baby. She had every right to report the child to Pharaoh, but she never did! What's more, Jochebed was the same person called as a midwife to nurse her own son. But now, she would be reaping the benefit of being a midwife to her son, who by custom of being a 'grandson' to Pharaoh, would be treated as a prince in a royal palace. Isn't it funny how sometimes God can use the very source of what is attacking to bless you?

Although, she may not be one of the more 'popular' female characters in the bible, this woman of God displayed a great demonstration of faith and determination. She completely shut out the noise of disaster and calamity going on around her. Let's put it in perspective, at the time of Pharaoh's decree of murder, she probably constantly heard the deafening weeping and wailing of mothers losing their sons, mass mourning's, funeral services, fights for those trying to defend their children from slaughter, the sound of people running about, trying to escape chaos and destruction. Despite this, she was not deterred and persisted to execute her plan, her faith and confidence in God, blocked out the fears and doubt. This persistence in God prepared her and positioned her in pursuit for the plan of God in her son's life to be established. The deeper revelation of this story is that the persistence of Jochebed was not directly for herself but for a life of another.

CHAPTER 3 PRAYER POINTS

1. Dear Father, reveal the power of prayer to me, give me the unquenchable desire to pray

2. Dear Father, help me to pray without ceasing, I will not just stop or give up in the place of prayer

3. Dear Father, may I regularly use my time to commune with you, help me be Consistent with my prayers

4. Dear Father, please give me the grace to pray persistently even when I don't see the answers immediately

EFFECTUAL PRAYERS

The essence of the word 'effectual' in summary can be explained as "sufficient to produce a desired result." When you pray, and it produces the desired result, then it is effectual. This would imply that not all prayers are effectual. Not all prayers are "sufficient to produce the desired result."

The prayer of a righteous person is powerful and effective. (James 5:16) I love the fact that the bible tries to lift us up and explain to us in verse 17 that Elijah was a man like we are, meaning he had issues too. In fact this is the same prophet Elijah who prayed for rain to stop pouring for three and a half years in Jerusalem and called down fire from heaven, but at the decree of a woman named Jezebel he went into hiding in the wilderness and began to have suicidal thoughts. What the bible is making us to understand is that even the great prophet Elijah is no different than you and me. Sometimes, when we read about these miraculous accounts in the Bible, we tend to lift them up and put the people who God used on a pedestal, forgetting that they are just men and women who are being used mightily by God.

At any moment, any time and at any place, we, as children of God have the privilege of approaching God in prayer. We can go to God with our requests; we go to him with our needs and our troubles. When we do, we hope that He hears and responds to our requests. It is of utmost importance that we do not think we are too small to be used by God. We too have the power to render effectual prayers to God. The sins of unbelief, of mistrust and of seeking help outside of God make prayer ineffectual. All things are possible for those who believe.

As we mature and grow in our prayer lives, the effectiveness of our prayer increases, our understanding of prayer changes, the kind of requests we make changes, our receptiveness and spiritual sensitivity becomes heightened.

"Becoming fervent or effectual in prayer is a maturing process; it a process that overtime shifts our focus from ourselves to God"

Also note, when looking at the miraculous story of Elijah calling down fire on top of mount Carmel, Elijah did not try and copy or mimic the behaviourisms of the prophets of Baal (they were cutting themselves, ranting raving and beating themselves) neither did he take it up as a competition between Himself and the prophets of Baal. He simply listened out for what God instructed him to do, focused on that and called upon the name of the Lord, trusting that He would answer. God does not ask for dramatics. God can ask you to do unusual things, but God does not need theatrics in order to answer our prayers. He wants our prayers to be fervent, to be heartfelt and filled with faith and trust in Him. So what makes our prayers effectual?

Asking God for Help

If my people, which are called by my name, shall humble themselves, and pray, and seek my face, and turn from their wicked ways; then will I hear from heaven, and will forgive their sin, and will heal their land'.

2 Chronicles 7:14. For most people, including myself, effectual prayer is not something that comes naturally. We often think we have everything figured out, which leads us to believe that we are better off doing things on our own without any input or help from the creator of all things. This belief prohibits us from reaching out to God and involving him in every aspect of our lives. I know in today's society, we are constantly reminded to be independent, to use our own initiative, trust no one, keep yourself to yourself, and be one step ahead of the game. However, God is asking the exact opposite, he is saying; "Trust me, depend on me, don't rely on your own understanding, I am with you always, acknowledge me in all your ways, cast your cares unto me, I want to take your heavy burden. I will go before you and make the crooked way straight." This is where we must put aside 'self' and surrender to God. Let Him help you.

As much as God has blessed us with amazing capabilities, gifts and talents, we cannot fulfil the plan and purpose of God for our lives on our own, we require God to help us. This is why the disciples asked "Lord, teach us to pray", they recognised that of themselves they could not accomplish what was necessary in accordance with God's will. They saw the phenomenal results of prayer in the life of Christ and his total dependence on God through prayer, as true disciples they also wanted to do the same. What about you? Do you depend on God through your prayer life? Do you trust that He can help you to align with His plan and purpose? Do you believe in His ability to bring about amazing results?

In the bible, a man named Nehemiah first fasted and prayed and sought God's help in the face of his country's ongoing demise and annihilation. As he did so, God revealed His plan and reversed years of deterioration over the course of a few days. This is because prayer saves time. In fact, you and I could save a lot of time and worry if we spent time praying first. God does not like being last. If prayer comes last, then so will the solution to the problem. We must not only talk about prayer but pray. Not only agree on the importance of prayer but pray. Not only preach on the power of prayer but pray.

"Prayer is an earthly request for heavenly intervention"

It is the weapon and armour we have been given to battle with and to pull out the invisible into the visible. However, we can't enjoy this kind of divine intervention if we never ask for it, once we come to understand that God's desire is to help us, the next step is simple; ask.

Using His Word

My Dad is a very powerful prayer warrior; I first learned how to pray through him. Growing up, one of the things I would watch him do is take a chapter or passage of the bible, it could be like 10-15 verses long but he would break down each verse and deduce a prayer point from there, he could even bring out 2 or 3 prayer points from the same verse. He would proclaim and declare the promises of God through the scriptures. He would tell me that the Word of God is power and it is our greatest spiritual weapon on earth. He would quote 2 Corinthians 10:3-6 'For though we walk in the flesh, we do not war after the flesh, For the weapons of our warfare are not carnal, but mighty through God to the pulling down of strong holds'. In this, I understood that we use the word of God to overcome and combat those things that try to exalt itself above the knowledge of God in our lives.

Jesus did the same, when he was tempted by Satan in the wilderness (Luke 4:1-12). Although He was the Son of God and he could have used his divine authority and just banished Satan, instead, he used the authority of the Word of God. Praying Scripture gives us authority over Satan. We will only be able to gain knowledge of these promises, gifts and authority when we become intimately familiar with the Bible. When we read these bible passages and pray along with it, the Holy Spirit can give us ideas and direction. Taking time to study His word is also a way we can show God that we truly desire His help. Scripture makes prayer simple. It literally gives us the words to say. My dad would tell me that there is no scripture in the bible that cannot be turned into a prayer point. Even the shortest verse in the bible like 'Jesus Wept' is a prayer point, 'O Lord give us the heart of compassion for your children, may we be moved with deep empathy for others who are hurting, suffering with the burden of loss and pain,' or 'O Lord, it is written; For we do not have a high priest who is unable to sympathise with our weaknesses, and we know because it says in your word Jesus Wept, you understand our sorrows and struggles, we pray in your compassion that you would heal and help us, so that your name alone will be glorified.' That's the thing about praying and using the scripture, you could have one scripture in mind and then another one is brought to your remembrance. Often, I find that you end up with a beautiful collection of God's words for your life. When we don't know what to do or even how to pray about situations and challenges that come our way, praying Scripture helps us to pray in a way that is pleasing to God. The word of God gives us the conversation material for our prayer lives which makes prayer easier and more enjoyable. We also gain much clarity and renewed strength, and we speak and pray God's Truth back to Him. This takes us into a deeper level of communion with Him.

Faith

The way of the world is to see first and then believe. The way of God is to believe first and then see. "Now faith is the substance of things hoped for, the evidence of things not seen". In other words, faith brings about the unseen things; it is the very thing that causes those things hoped for to come into being. In the verses that follow Hebrews 11:1, the writer goes ahead to bring out different believers who understood the essence of having faith in God. Each character demonstrated their trust and assurance that God would act according to His promises. The "assurance" and "conviction" of faith is not naivety, or blind belief or wishful thinking. Their "faith" was not accepting fantasies and folk tales; it was acting in full confidence that God would do as He had promised, based on their knowledge and experience of God. The reason why someone can be called a Christian today is because they truly believe in the death, resurrection and authority of Jesus Christ. Faith is at the very heart of Christianity, which is the first basis. As you continue to walk with God, you will soon realise that **faith is a lifelong process; it is a commitment to rely on the knowledge of God and in His goodness that we have gained in the past, while reaching for additional knowledge and assurance in our**

future. As we grow in our faith and put faith to work, it becomes confidence, and finally when it becomes fully operational, it is trust. This trust is realised because of the full measure of faith.

For our prayers to be effective, we must first believe that God is listening, he hears our prayers, and is capable of giving us all that is in accordance to His will. You might ask 'but how can we be sure that our request will be given especially as we do not always know the will of God?' The truth is that we may not always know if what we are asking for is aligning with God's will, therefore we must pray; pray for His guidance, pray for the holy spirit to align your will with the Father's will. Although you may want a particular thing, be sure to surrender your wants, needs and desires to the Father, trusting that He will give to you what is good and not evil. The stories of the biblical characters cited in Hebrews 11, should inspire confidence in us that God will fulfil His promises. God "creates" out of things we cannot see, just as He created the heavens and the earth out of complete nothingness.

One of the vital ways to achieve this confidence and trust is to constantly remain in His word, in doing so; faith in God becomes part of our thinking and conduct. *"So, then faith comes by hearing, and hearing by the word of God."* Hearing His word and taking it in, helps us to understand the will of God better and shapes our prayers in line with the plan and purpose of God for our lives. Faith includes a mixture of believing, knowing, understanding and sometimes having bold and daring conviction in God. Many claim to believe in God, yet still their belief has little to no influence in their daily lives. This is also reflective in their prayer life; such people are always unsure, and without full conviction.

"Such are those who seek lucky breaks instead of the Lord's breakthroughs"

Such belief is without certainty, and so after small time it gradually rescinds, *"But he must ask in faith, without doubting, because he who doubts is like a wave of the sea, blown and tossed by the wind. That man should not expect to receive anything from the Lord"*. The answer is literally in the text. Verse 7 says *"such person should not expect to receive anything from the Lord"*. Faith and understanding in God, this is what produces an effectual prayer life. You cannot receive anything through prayer if you do not first believe.

Faith is something that continually grows and matures through our prayer experiences. We come to know that we have authority over all things through Christ Jesus and through our faith-based prayers. Jesus said that He has given us authority over every principalities, powers and attacks of the enemy. However we must understand that knowing scripture is not to be equated with believing, they are not the same thing. Believing comes from seeing our prayers change things. The more we practice prayer, the more we build up our faith. Faith should be treated like a musical instrument; it takes practice, just like with anything in life. If you don't use it inevitably you'll lose it. We can't please God without using our faith; it is like a magnet that draws God's attention to our prayers. When you pray, you need to believe that God will answer your prayer; it takes faith to pray effectual prayers.

Obedience

When it comes to our relationship with God, I think most of us like to think we would do whatever God asks us to do and sometimes we sing this out in our songs and worship to him; but when it comes to the practicality of our complete obedience to Him, things become quite different. We become negotiators and seasoned defence lawyers. In prayer, we are willing to say, "I will do what you want me to do God, if you come through for me. I will obey you and follow your commandments if you bless my finances. If you bless me with a new job, I will go to church more often and read my morning devotions". Then after God has blessed us we begin to argue our case for and against as to why we are not fit for the tasks he has assigned to us. We must understand that obedience to the commandments of God is a prerequisite and key factor in producing effectual prayers to God.

I would go as far as saying that obedience to God is single-handedly the most effectual tool in prayer. How can anyone go wrong when they are in direct obedience to God? When I read the Bible, I see so many amazing and miraculous stories as a result of obedience. However, I have come to realise that we as a people, don't obey enough to experience those amazing stories ourselves. In the Bible, we see that Jesus, the only perfect person who ever walked this Earth, was always praying and in total obedience to God. Obeying God is a wonderful experience; however, it is an aspect of the Christian walk that many of us struggle with. Admittedly, it can be quite scary to let go and allow someone else to take control of our lives. This is where the scripture Psalms 3:15 is useful. *'Trust in the Lord with all your heart and lean not on your own understandings; in all thy ways acknowledge him and he shall direct your path.'* Many things can easily shift our trust from God. Yet, once we learn to totally trust him, our experience and results will be greater. Early on in my Christian journey, I assumed that I knew what was best for me. I would make my prayer requests known to God followed by a quick and lacklustre, not my will but your prayer to round it off because that was the thing to say. The problem was my hardened heart was not willing to submit; I discovered that true submission doesn't always come naturally. In order to bring your heart in submission to God, you must pray! There is no way around it; there are things that by virtue of our human nature remains difficult to do. In Matthew 26:41 it says '.... *the spirit is willing, but the flesh is weak'*. Jesus, himself, our greatest example taught us how to submit to God by giving us "The Lord's Prayer." In it we are instructed to ask that God's will be done.

All power has been given unto Jesus and He in turn has passed that power to us. This power, however, is not immediately available to us; there is a process in which we may come across challenges that cause us to make a decision; like Joseph, who was tempted by a very beautiful woman of influence Potiphar's wife, yet he chose to obey God. The decision to obey God is not always the easiest, but without doubt has far greater rewards; When King Saul disobeyed God's instruction, Prophet Samuel told him; *'Hath the LORD as great delight in burnt offerings and sacrifices, as in obeying the voice of the LORD? Behold, to obey is better than sacrifice, and to hearken than the fat of rams. For rebellion is as the sin of witchcraft, and stubbornness is as iniquity and idolatry. Because thou hast rejected the word of the LORD, he hath also rejected thee from being king.'* (1 Sam. 15:22-23). Saul, in his disobedience, rejected the word of the Lord, and once God's words are rejected, you, in essence, are also rejecting God. God honours His word more than His name; therefore, GOD also honours those who honour His word. Would God honour the prayers of a liar and rebellious person? Not likely.

John gave us the answer by saying, *"He that saith, I know him, and keepeth not his commandments, is a liar, and the truth is not in him"* (1 John 2:4).   John explains that, if you do not keep God's commandment, not only are you lying, but you don't really know God at all. In the next chapter, John spells out what makes prayers answerable; *"And whatsoever we ask, we receive of him, because we keep his commandments, and do those things that are pleasing in his sight"* (1 John 3:22). The one who listens and obeys God's commands is a true lover of God, if you listen, you must also obey. Without obedience, the Christian believer is wasting his or her time in the place of prayer. Jesus said: *"If you love me, keep my commandments."* Our obedience to God shows God that we truly love him and enables us to execute the power and authority Jesus has acquired for us. This is the foundation of a powerful prayer life.

Fervent Prayers

When I think about fervent prayers, I think about the word 'intensity'. I looked up the word and it is defined as the quality of being very strong, concentrated or difficult, or the degree to which something is difficult or strong. An example of intensity is having the ability to run for miles on end at top speed. Now imagine that in terms of prayer, your prayers travelling at top speed to reach God Almighty. It gives you a clear link to God whilst giving you a faster connection, in today's terms it would be the equivalent of swapping to fibre optic broadband or the 5G wireless network for faster internet access. Intensity is also often linked to passion. When we pray we must be passionate about what we are praying about. We should not be apathetic and rigid. We must mean business; we simply cannot afford to be nonchalant. This kind of prayer can be seen in the life of Jacob who actually tells God; *"I will not let you go unless you bless me."* This is the kind of fervency and intensity we need in our prayer lives. Jacob was saying, "You can't do anything to stop me now, no matter how rough and tough it is, even if I must fight. I am holding on till all that you promised me is fulfilled in my life.

If we were invited to present a request before the Queen of England, I think most of us would ensure that our speech was filled with enthusiasm, reverence and clarity and much more. Then why do we feel that God does not require the same eagerness and reverence? Consistent effectual prayer is not a routine; it is our life line, our survival. It is crucial to winning the battles of life and overcoming the biggest battle of all which is our very selves. Jesus was also fervent with his prayers. He knew that He needed help from God to go through the ordeal of dying on the cross. In the garden of Gethsemane, he had to pray and submit his own will and desires to God. This was no ordinary prayer; the bible depicts the passion and struggle of the prayer being so intense that Christ's sweat was like drops of blood. Now I am not insinuating that we should produce sweat like blood from our bodies in order for God to answer our prayers, what I am insinuating is that we must ensure that we are intentional with our prayers, we must be willing to make the sacrifice of prayer before God, In other words, 'tarry before the Lord'. In fact, Jesus was unimpressed with his disciples in Matthew 34:44 when they could not 'tarry'. 'Jesus returned to the disciples and found them sleeping. *"Were you not able to keep watch with me for one hour?" He asked Peter'*. So also, I ask the same question to you, 'Can you keep watch with Christ in prayer?'

This is Christ's most fervent prayer session recorded during the duration of his ministry. Interestingly, the prayer was not about anything material, nor was it even about his friends; it was solely for the purpose of God to be fulfilled through His life. I believe this part was recorded to highlight the lengths to which we may have to go in order to subdue our flesh and align with the will of God which can only be accomplished when we become FERVENT with our prayers.

Those who experienced answers to fervent prayers were never the same again; Jabez was one of these people who brought intense prayers before God. *"Oh, that you would bless me and enlarge my border, and that your hand might be with me, and that you would keep me from harm so that it might not bring me pain! And God granted what he asked".* Jabez was passionately crying out to the Lord, in fact it is one of the most astonishing prayers I have come across in the bible. It really is a person simply understanding who His father is and requesting for His help. Jabez was intentional and forthright in his prayers believing God would answer. There was no ceremony, ritual or steps needed, merely a simple heartfelt dialogue between father and son. In Romans 12:11 we are advised not be slothful in business; but instead be *"fervent in spirit serving the Lord".* The truth is we cannot be lazy with our prayers; we must be intentional and passionate about them. It cannot be effective if done in any other manner; effective prayer requires effort.

CHAPTER 4 PRAYER POINTS

1. Dear Father, bring to my remembrance your holy words as I lift up my requests to you

2. Dear Father, fill me up with the intensity and fervency in the place of prayer

3. Dear Father, increase my faith, so that I might believe in the prayers that I release in accordance with your will

4. Dear Father, Give me the grace to obey your commandments and to show my love to you

ARE YOU RIGHTEOUS?

Awhile back, around the time I received the revelation for this book, I took to Facebook and posted this; "We quote the scripture... the prayer of a righteous man availeth much. The real question is, are you righteous? If you can't answer the question, then you can now see why your prayers are not availing.' I posted this on my wall not realising the magnitude of what I had written. Being righteous and living a righteous life is the 'the fuel' to effective prayers. 1 Peter 3:12 states; *For the eyes of the Lord are over the righteous, and his ears are open unto their prayers: but the face of the Lord is against them that do evil"*. It is the effectual fervent prayer of a righteous man that avails much. Simply put, God answers the prayers of those who have a right standing with Him, who like Him are Holy. Such a person lives a life that is pleasing to God; they put God as the number one priority and surrender solely to His will. If we look at the lives of Moses, David, Joseph, Esther, Mary, Lydia, the apostles and so many others, you will see that they lived a life of righteousness; this is not to say that they lived a perfect life without faults, but in their actions and deeds they strived to be Holy. They ensured they fulfilled all righteousness, at times that could have meant looking foolish or even at the cost of their lives, but they remained strong in the faith, that God had given them the ability to be a true reflection of Him.

To find out how to be righteous, we must first look at what righteousness is. Righteousness is defined in the Cambridge English dictionary as someone who is morally correct. To be morally correct is described as someone who is concerned with the principles of right and wrong behaviour, or someone who holds strong principles for what they consider proper comportment.

This is the definition most people tend to connect with and interpret as having a long list of rules that they follow religiously whilst monitoring how well they are getting along in comparison to other people. News Flash! This is NOT the righteousness of God; this is righteousness of self.

Self-righteousness is not what God desires from us. Jesus reprimands the Pharisees for this type of behaviour. In (Matthew 23:27–28) Jesus describes what self-righteousness looks like, he says to them, *"Woe to you, teachers of the law and Pharisees, you hypocrites! You are like whitewashed tombs, which look beautiful on the outside but on the inside are full of the bones of the dead and everything unclean. In the same way, on the outside, you appear to people as righteous but, on the inside, you are full of hypocrisy and wickedness".* Self-righteous is primarily concerned with how you appear on the outside without addressing what is happening on the inside, which is contrary to what real righteousness in God is. I once heard righteousness explained as "the condition of being acceptable to God as made possible by God". This to me is one of the simplest and most profound definitions of righteousness. It emphasises that the righteousness you have doesn't actually have anything to do with you. Even if seemingly we are following His commandments and laws, the truth is that no amount of man-made effort will result in righteousness.

"The word righteous certainly does not refer to a quality of man; the righteous are those who are clothed with grace"

Therefore no one is too weak or too unworthy to be righteous, a righteous person has a heart that seeks God's will and truth. Such heart will continually be renewed by the word of God. Just like David realised in the book of Psalm 119:11, he declared that he had hidden God's word in his heart that he might not sin against Him. This is the same attitude that we are to have, that desire and yearning to meditate in the word of God daily and become Holy as the Lord is Holy.

For us to even pursue the righteousness of God, we must first recognise that we cannot please God with our sinful behaviour. The idea that you can sin and still please God is false and categorically demonic in nature. Paul expressly addressed this in Romans 6:1-2, when he asks and answers his own question to the church of Antioch, *'Can we continue in sin and ask for the grace of God to abound? Absolutely not'!* The danger of some of the teachings that is being spread around today is that God is simply okay with our sins as long as we sing a couple of worship songs, hold a position in the church, help a few people and have a positive influence in society. This is false. This is why many believers and Churches are so weak in the faith, with many falling away to witchcraft, demonic practices, sexual misconducts, pursuit of money instead of souls and living in perpetual sin. Week after week they come back to church dancing and shouting; yet nothing happens, nothing changes. They stay the same. Why? Because believers have no genuine commitment to living a life that pleases God. Living alternative lives renders the Church powerless to truly heal or save anyone. Miracles, signs and wonders are not just a once in a lifetime conference or two-day event experience. We are called to walk in the supernatural daily as long as believers are living sinful lifestyles in secret or openly, they will never experience the fullness of the Holy Spirit, nor will they have the power and anointing to break yokes through prayer.

God holds us in high esteem, irrespective of what position we hold or the denomination of church we go to. He expects us to uphold his holy standard. We are called out of darkness into His marvellous light. God is looking for Righteous men and women in our world today. My question to you is; will you be that Righteous person? You may look at this question and think to yourself, but how? How can I be righteous? What does that entail?

Set apart

One of the qualities God is looking for is people set apart for His glory. We are to separate ourselves from things that are not Godly. We are to come out of darkness and come into God's marvellous light. In the scriptures, it states that we are from the world, but we are not of the world. Though we are born into an environment, we are not inherently products of that environment. We are God's children and ambassadors for him, here on earth. This means we do things that please God, reverencing him in all that we do. We are Holy just as our Father in heaven is holy. I remember when I was younger, and I always wanted to be like everyone else and do what everyone else was doing, my dad would constantly say to me, 'Bea, you are different, you can't do that, you're not like the others'. I used to get so irritated by this reminder, I would say to myself but what about if I want to be the same as everyone else, until I realised the more that I tried to fit in, the more my difference became more apparent.

Moses is someone who struggled with his true identity, born a Hebrew slave, but brought up in an Egyptian palace, the reality was that he didn't fit in either world. In his actions, we see that he wanted to fulfil the purpose for which God has rescued Him (from the death warrant of Pharaoh). He seemed to have a vague indication of what his purpose was, but he failed in its application, which led to his wilderness experience. For many of us, we have some understanding that we are called to be different, but we just don't know how to go about it. Admittedly, this can be difficult, frustrating and even damaging to us and others. When Moses discovered himself and became set apart and came out from among his influences and learned how to properly live out for God despite all his imperfections, He was able to carry out what God wanted him to, God was glorified, and the people of Israel were delivered.

The same is true in our lives. He wants to lead us to Holiness and consecration by His Word and through the Holy Spirit. God has laid out his guidelines for our lives in Scripture; that should be our first standard for living. Those who follow these guidelines are those God sets apart for His service and glory. Things set apart are holy things, just like Moses, when a believer matures and becomes set apart, the believer then becomes sanctified for the Master's use.

Sanctification

Sanctification derives from the Hebrew word 'Quadosh'; which means things set apart for the worship of God. This is the process in which we, as believers, become surrendered and set apart for God's use. Sanctified believers are people who refuse to be drawn in by the dysfunction and seductions of sin; this is not to say they do not encounter sin; but when they do, they retain the understanding that they cannot be affiliated or associated with unholy things. This reminds me of the lightbulb moment experienced by the prodigal son, when he came to the realisation that he was a son, who had a father. At that moment he knew he was different; he could no longer dwell and remain in such filthy place with swine. He took himself out of that environment and back to His father's house where he always belonged. As believers, we must realise that we are sons and daughters of God. We are sanctified, we are called clean and therefore we cannot be unclean. We cannot allow ourselves to be carried away by lust, sins and unsound doctrines of men. It is important for us to be deeply rooted in the Word of God. When we have the word of God in us, we will not be deceived by the enticing words of sin. Having such a sanctified mentality helps us to be uncompromising in our faith. When we begin to think in this way, we begin to live to glorify God alone. We become filled with the Holy Spirit and power and then, of course, we have a prayerful life, which brings effectual results.

At a time such as this, God is searching for men and women who would abstain from all appearances of things that are sinful, lustful and evil. Now, to most that may sound like it's impossible, but that's why we have to rely on a God who specialises in the impossibilities. For in His word, he says that *with men this is impossible, but with God all things are possible.'* Now, usually people use this verse to talk about goals, achievements and material things. However, I believe God is talking about us conforming into His likeness. The amazing thing about this is, we have the help of the Holy Spirit as written in Acts 2:38, 'He tells us to "walk in the Spirit"'. The full verse states that when we walk in the spirit, we will not fulfil the lusts of the flesh. Walking in the Spirit means we live a life of total surrender to the Lordship of Jesus Christ; we cultivate the ability to hear God and the habit of obeying His voice in all that we do. Once this becomes our habitual lifestyle, we become inclined to the character of Christ and desire holiness more than fleshly indulgence, such awareness brings about humility. As we begin to spend more time in the presence of God, we become more aware of our own sins and shortcomings. An off-white shirt may look fully white alongside a dark wall, however in comparison with snow, the same shirt looks dirty. Likewise, the issues of pride and self-righteousness cannot masquerade in God's presence. He will show us the things that we need to let go of and remove, exposing every spot, blemish, wrinkle, and even what we believe to be 'white' in our own eyes. Understand that He does this not to judge or condemn; but for us to be transformed into the likeness of His son.

Fulfilling Righteousness

Those who are set apart and sanctified are believers who commit themselves to God's word. Such people do not just fold their hands; they continually seek first the kingdom of God and His righteousness. These kinds of believers know they have nothing, everything they have belongs to God; a life set apart, a peculiar life, cleansed, purged, and sanctified to produce good works of faith. James says, *"faith without works is dead."* Now this is completely different from someone who is not born again, who says I am a good man or woman. A person who claims he or she knows the Lord should have the works of righteousness displayed through them. The Bible says, *"by their fruits ye shall know them."* You can't claim to be a child of God when you are committing adultery, living in fornication, stealing and cheating. You are like the blind, leading the blind.

Instead, God is looking for people who walk in communicable relationship with Him and trust His Words, even when they don't fully understand it, even when the world laughs and mocks them. These are resilient people who persevere in obedience to God despite all odds and hardships; these are the people who, in all they do, glorify the Lord.

In all honesty, I, at one time, believed this to be unattainable; I thought to myself we can never fulfil the righteousness of God on earth until I revisited the life of David. The bible narrates the story of how David went from the rugged-shepherd boy to David, a man after God's own heart'. David is a perfect role model for us; he was an ordinary man with some of the struggles that many of us still struggle with today; setbacks, discouragements, being a wanted criminal, a refugee, feelings of lust, envy and greed. But we can learn something about how he orchestrated his steps, the kind of behaviour and attitude he displayed to embrace the path of God's righteousness. Psalm 1:1-3 states *'How blessed is the man who does not walk in the counsel of the wicked, nor stand in the path of sinners, nor sit in the seat of scoffers! But his delight is in the law of the lord, and in His law, he meditates day and night. He will be like a tree firmly planted, by streams of water, which yields its fruit in its season and its leaf does not wither; and in whatever he does, he prospers'*. This scripture can be reflective in David's life regarding his commitment to God's Word *"...his delight is in the law of the Lord..."*and *"...in His law he meditates day and night."* It was part of his prayer life and spiritual walk; he consistently and consciously set himself apart from what was evil and contrary to God. He studied and occupied his thoughts and time with God's word every single day.

As a result, David had an unshakeable spiritual foundation *"like a tree firmly planted* "which was constantly nurtured by the Spirit *"streams of water"*. This, therefore, allowed him to live a fruitful life; *"yields fruit in its season"*, and although he had been through the valleys of the shadow of death, his situation changed and sometimes went from bad to worse. But his commitment to God did not; *"its leaf does not wither"*. He did not just stop at one victory or one answered prayer. He continued to mature and grow spiritually throughout his life; *"in whatever he does, he prospers"*. David followed and pursued the word of God which allowed him to receive the full benefits of being a child of God. He also understood the indiscipline that ensues when one does not commit themselves to God's Word. by not having the counsel of God's Word, they *"walk in the counsel of the wicked"*. Not obtaining the insight and wisdom provided by God's Word, they *"sit in the seat of scoffers"*. The characteristics of a righteous woman or godly man is someone in good spiritual standing with God. I absolutely love the example of David's life because he was committed to regular prayer; he understood the nature and substance of that commitment. Throughout the book of Psalms, we can capture a glimpse of this commitment in which each day begun with open and honest conversations with God. In the latter part of (Psalm 5:3), David declares, *"I will order my prayer"*. It is a way of saying that he will pray with directives, intent and reverence as well as adhering to the right attitudes that are pleasing to God.

This is how we should all relate and come before God in prayer. People that bring their prayers to God while allowing wrong behaviours to continue in their life such as lying, jealousy, sexual immorality, wickedness, greed, boasting and deceit will not be heard by God because He cannot accept the impure condition of their hearts before Him. Just as the Old Testament sacrifices did not actually remove sin for those following the rituals without a changed heart, likewise prayer that is given without a repentant and submissive heart, has no effect.

CHAPTER 5 PRAYER POINTS

1. Dear Father, I rest in your righteousness and not the rules of morality I place on myself, help me to walk in true righteousness

2. Dear Father, give me the grace and strength to separate myself from the things that are not of God

3. Dear Father, sanctify me so that I can be used for your plan and purpose on earth,

4. Dear Father, may I walk in the spirit and not in the flesh, fulfilling all righteousness through Christ Jesus

HINDRANCES TO PRAYER

Sometimes our prayers are hindered and not answered; this could be as a result of many different things. Sometimes it could be because we pray for selfish reasons that are not in line with the will of God. Sometimes it's because we have no idea who we are praying to. Sometimes it's because we pray but do not believe we will receive what we are praying for. I do not know if you can relate, but prayer has not always been something that I have enthusiastically wanted to do. It's like my **flesh rebels against this spiritual activity which dethrones fleshly cravings**. I can remember when I was 12; boldly telling my Nigerian aunt after a prayer meeting, that prayer is nothing short of 'boring'. 'Phew'! What can I say, I was a bold kid. But like so many others I had not yet grasped the depths of prayer because I had no close relationship with God at the time. I could not appreciate the potency of its power. Throughout the pages of the Bible, we see example after example of men and women who prayed to God and saw the supernatural; the miracles, signs and wonders. I know I should too, but I often found this challenging, I still do and I suspect I am not alone. There are many reasons and there could even be a combination of reasons why these hindrances occur, but what we must understand is that we have one common enemy, whose main objective is to keep Christians weak and feeble. He knows that we have the power of prayer to keep us in line with God's will and to triumph over every situation that presents itself before us.

From the beginning of time, **it has always been the devil's mission to take every child of God out of God's love**. In the beginning with Adam and Eve, the devil deceived them;

subsequently they found themselves out of both the presence and away from the love of God. The trick remains the same; the devil is still trying to pull the veil of darkness over every believer so that we will not understand who God is and all that He has for us. His primary way of hindering a believer is stopping you from praying and hindering the process of prayer. Our Lord Jesus taught us to pray, "Father, deliver us from the Evil One," and by saying that, Jesus clearly indicates that the devil has plans to capture us and hinder us in our walk with God, and generally cause us harm. This doesn't mean that we should be afraid in any way because Jesus Christ has given us total victory and authority over the devil and when we being righteous, pray according to God's will, we witness the extraordinary impact and miraculous power of God.

Most Christians generally see prayer as an important component of their relationship with God. We can bring our worries and troubles to our Father, we can ask for anything in Jesus's name, we can be confident in our approach to God because of the blood of Jesus and the redemption of the cross. So how is it that we can be so easily deceived and diverted from prayer? Well, for a start, we are just mere mortals; prone to sin, easily distractible and not yet transformed into glory. The devil too knows that prayer is our strongest weapon, our weapon of mass destruction towards His kingdom and activities. Therefore, just like any enemy amidst war, he will try every means necessary to disable his opponents and render them weak and powerless before issuing a full-on attack. An army expert will tell you that one of the main ways to destabilise an army is to attack their source of power; this could be economically, through basic amenities like food and water, and their supply of weapons. Once you can take hold of any of these, you have an advantage over your opponent. This is exactly what the devil tries to achieve with us as believers; he takes advantage of our less-than-perfect features, and constantly tries to deceive us.

In the Garden of Eden, Satan starts out by appealing to a distortion of the truth, grounding his lies in something that is easy to believe. With Eve, he works with the situation at hand; the fruit of the tree looks good to eat, *"Did God actually say, 'You shall not eat of any tree in the garden'?"* (Genesis 3:1). This is why it is crucial to meditate and digest the word of God. I cannot emphasise this enough, the devil comes to manipulate and distort the word of God, which is how he gets the believers trapped in deceit, because they are not entirely sure of God's word, nor do they have full confidence in it. Now that the devil has you unsure of God's word, he introduces the lie; *"You will not surely die"* (Genesis 3:4), followed by an attractive suggestion that is contrary to the will of God: *"You will be like God"* (Genesis 3:5).

This is the devil's consistent approach to contradict the truth and twist it out of shape, so that it appears to be something worth believing. This is the same way he lies to us about prayer. 'Prayer doesn't really do much, so why bother? I mean, it's not like it does anything anyway. It's just a means to make you feel better about your life." Thoughts like 'Prayer just makes you feel better' is too small a view of prayer, this kind of view occurs when you haven't really grasped the full picture of How Mighty, Powerful and Sovereign God is. A too-small view of God creates a too-small view of prayer. Such small views is in direct conflict with the scriptures (John 14:13-14) *"Whatever you ask in my name, this I will do, that the Father may be glorified in the Son. If you ask me anything in my name, I will do it."* The bible states that he will do whatever we ask in his name, with clear words that God is able to do it, so our act of asking as believers is therefore effective.

Another one of the devil's deceptions that hinders us from prayer is this idea that 'I'm too busy? Whenever, I find myself in this frame of thinking that I am too busy to pray I ask myself, am I too busy to eat? Am I too busy to shower? Visit friends? Watch movies/news/TV? Getting distracted from prayer because of other things is one of the easiest things, especially in this social media era. In the midst of that, you hear in your mind, "God knows your heart; he knows that you need to get through these tasks. Prayer can wait." There's a real discipline in setting aside time to pray, in fact for any relationship to thrive, it is crucial for time to be created. Running out of time and therefore neglecting prayer because you spent too long talking to your friends or working or scrolling through Instagram/Facebook is not exercising the authority and power given to us through Jesus Christ.

What can you do to overcome these distractions? Pray! Yes, pray now! Don't put it off and get distracted and forget. If necessary, put this book down now and go pray. Prayer should be our first response, not our last resort. It is a priority. *'Now when Daniel learned that the decree had been published, he went home to his upstairs room where the windows opened toward Jerusalem. Three times a day he got down on his knees and prayed, giving thanks to his God, just as he had done before.'* (The first has the power to bless the rest, so make prayer a priority by making it the first thing you do before anything else. It gets God's attention when He is your priority, and then it sets the precedent for everything that follows.

Sin

But I do pray! The problem is not that I do not pray, the issue is when I do, my prayers are not being answered. Why? This is a question that I have asked myself time and time again. Whilst there are many answers to this query, I have discovered that one of the main reasons of unanswered prayers can be likened to any telephone conversation. Having a good and clear line helps immensely when speaking to another person, the accuracy of the information passed through the telephone can be hindered simply by the type of connection that person has. If you have a bad signal, it disrupts the line, in fact, at some point it can become extremely difficult for you to hear each other. You may begin to hear the other caller intermittently. At times, the phone line simply disconnects, and even when you try to re-dial and reconnect, the line fails to connect to the other phone user. Likewise, if you harbour sin in your life (the bad signals) and continue to walk in contrast to God's plan and purpose for your life, your phone will keep cutting out and invariably will be disconnected. That is why our lifestyles matter when it comes to prayer.

There are numerous scriptures which indicate that it is impossible to be in sin and still receive answers from God. It is a very strange notion to believe that you can continue in sin and still expect answers to your prayers. Even as a parent, if your child continually disobeys every time you ask them to do something, a good parent would not then reward the child with their request. In Isaiah 59:1-2, it states *"Behold, the LORD'S hand is not shortened, that it cannot save; neither his ear heavy that it cannot hear: But your iniquities have separated between you and your God, and your sins have hid his face from you, that he will not hear"*. This verse expressly implies that prayers can be hindered by sin; Christians must endeavour to live in a way that does not hinder their prayers. The way of prayer to God involves a conscious exertion. It is not just by our words to God but through our actions to Him and to others. All prayers are a product of relationship, but the depth of our relationship can limit what we are able to receive from Him. God is a lover and He delights in our "connections" with Him. However, sin will deprive the believer from God's connection. *"Seek the Lord while He may be found, call upon Him while He is near. Let the wicked forsake His ways and the unrighteous man his thoughts. Let him return unto the Lord, and He will have mercy upon him and to our God, He will abundantly pardon."* (Isaiah 55: 6-8).

You will never have true power with God or men if you live in sin. You will never be anointed or filled with the power of the Holy Spirit, for holiness is power. Slowly and eventually if sin continues, the believer will be deprived of eternal life. God hates sin, whether out in the open or hidden in secret, whether you are a bishop, pastor or church attendee, there are no ifs, buts or maybes. Sin puts a strain on our relationship with God. It is a breach. It causes us to run from God instead of seeking help from him; just like Adam and Eve hiding from God in the Garden of Eden with their makeshift clothing made from leaves and figs. When we sin, we become ashamed and likewise hide. We hide behind our schedules, hobbies, family responsibilities, goals, or even ministry. It is important therefore to see how sin affects our relationship with God. Even prayerlessness is mostly a manifestation of sin and its effects. However, prayer is also the cure, Oh the irony! The very thing we struggle to do is what is required to overcome the struggle. It is the only way out. Prayer brings about clarity and exposes our weaknesses before God. This is why even when we don't feel like it, we must still pray! The way to come out of sin and its power is to confess it and repent, knowing with full assurance that God will forgive us. What you must understand is sin fundamentally is pride. It is an act that insinuates that for whatever reason you know better. Prayer, at its core, is the direct opposite. It is an act of humility, expressing that you do not know, and therefore surrender to the one that does. Therefore, the only way out of sin is to humble ourselves before God. How do we do that? It's simple. We Pray.

Unbelief

We've all struggled at some point in our life with worry and doubt. As Christians, the bible tells us to have no anxiety about anything, but in everything by prayer and supplication with thanksgiving, we should let our requests be made known to God. And the peace of God, which passes all understanding, will keep your hearts and your minds in Christ Jesus. (Philippians 4:6-7) How do we truly not worry about anything? This seems pretty impossible! However, I discovered that to doubt is to think about problems and potential outcomes, especially because we think something negative might happen. If you look at some of the synonyms of worry, you might get a broader idea as to what it entails. In the English thesaurus, it links worrying to; apprehension, uneasiness, fear, anxiety, burden, disquiet and unrest. Immediately in these definitions, we see that there is no positive outcome, from the meanings and examples provided, not an iota of hope is found. Also, notice how worry presumes that we anticipate a negative outcome to the situation we are thinking about. All these meanings about worry contradict the meaning of prayer and faith. When we pray, we have hope and trust that God will work these things out together for our good. We pray to Him because we know that He has control over the situation. Through prayer, we can realise certain things. One is that perhaps the problem I am concerned about is not really mine. Since it is not mine to control, I need to let it go because it is robbing me of my peace.

Billy Graham wrote in 1965, 'at its best, anxiety distracts us from our relationship with God and the truth that He is "Lord of heaven and earth" (Matthew 11:25). At its worst, anxiety is a crippling disease, taking over our minds and plunging our thoughts into darkness.' Looking at this statement, this is where a lot of us find ourselves; we as a result of our worry and anxiety, forget who God is and what He has done for us in times past. Just like the Israelites in the book of Exodus, after God had delivered them from Egypt and the hands of Pharaoh at the Red Sea, they got to the wilderness and because they faced the worries of no bread and water they conceived in their minds that they would die of starvation. Thinking in this way undermines God's power and authority. What we are saying to God is that He is incapable of saving, delivering, healing and protecting us. It is at these points in our lives we need to understand who we are to God. That is why it is imperative as Christians to hold onto the Word of God. We need to refresh our minds with the fact that he is more than able to take care of and sort out the situation you are fretting over. He will give you wisdom, send helpers and open up closed doors. God wants so much more for us than to walk through life full of fear, worry and anxiety; *"For God hath not given us the spirit of fear; but of power, and of love, and of a sound mind"* (2 Timothy 2:17).

I came across a quote on Facebook at the beginning of the year, on the post it read, 'Do not forget in the darkness what God said to you in the light'. As soon as I saw it, it pierced my heart. It really struck me because I had been trusting God for a lot of things and not yet seen it manifesting, and therefore my faith in God waned, which I believe, happens to a lot of us. We read the bible, meditate on some scriptures, and praise God for his goodness. But when it comes to believing in the promises of God that He has for us, we retract and go back on all we have come to know about God. Doubt is like a cancer, which slowly eats away at your faith. Doubt is a product of fear and fear is in total opposition to faith.

This is our fundamental battle as Christians. We are challenged to overcome the flesh, the devil, and the world daily by exercising and reinforcing our faith. The "flesh" in this case refers to unbelief and doubt which are the enemies of every believer. We do not naturally believe in God's love for us, because we have never known unconditional love. Our doubt and unbelief separates us from God and blames Him for whatever state we find ourselves in. This is the nature and work of the devil, when we oppose his works in our actions and through our prayers, we are actually fighting the devil by bringing the blessing of God to people who often have been cheated out of it. We must be careful because the enemy has deceived us into fearing the will of God. We operate out of this false belief that God doesn't want what's best for us. We believe that full trust and belief in God will result in our disappointment and demise. This is not the truth. This false belief leads us to believe that we know better than God. We don't ask that God's will be done because we do not believe that he is working all things together for our good. This is a serious misjudgement; it shows that we don't really know God and we don't understand the consequences of not having faith in of being outside of His will. Anytime we find ourselves outside the will of God, we are treading on a very dangerous territory, it means we are prey to the enemy and he is at liberty to do whatever terrible thing he pleases. A perfect example is Adam and Eve stepping outside the will of God, which resulted in the fall and death of Man. They found themselves outside the will of God because they allowed doubt to enter in. They were not fully confident in God's promises and instructions towards them in the Garden of Eden. God is a loving heavenly father who would and has sacrificed all for us. His character is love and we must truly know and understand; his plans for us are of good and not of evil. His love would not allow Him to do us harm. *Finally, brothers, whatever is true, whatever is honourable, whatever is just, whatever is pure, whatever is lovely, whatever is commendable, if there is any excellence, if there is anything worthy of praise, think about these things. "What you have learned and received and heard and seen in me, practice these things, and the God of peace will be with you"* (Philippians 4:8-9, ESV). This scripture is the solution to combating the likes of doubt, anxiety, and fear by renewing our minds with His words.

CHAPTER 6 PRAYER POINTS

1. Dear Father, help me to flee and overcome sin through prayer

2. Dear Father, teach me how to better utilise my time so that I can be 'busy' in the place of prayer

3. Dear Father, give me the understanding in the place of prayer, to know why my prayers are being hindered and the grace to address these hindrances

4. Dear Father, teach me how to use prayer and faith to combat doubt and anxiety, help my unbelief and increase my faith

FINAL WORDS

I want you all to know that with prayer, anything can happen. Circumstances can change, healing can take place, transformation is possible and your relationship with God can be even stronger and more defined. Prayer comes out of our relationship with God and it is in that relationship, we learn about prayer. There is more to learn about prayer and it is not just something to say, nor is it just an activity, but a journey and a lifelong commitment.

Prayers that do not avail are disappointments to us and often bruise our faith and confidence in prayer. In fact, people have ended their relationship with God because they blame Him for not answering an important prayer. When our prayers are not answered, sometimes we feel like all of this is pointless and even for those who know His love and blessings in many other areas quietly wonder "why". But God wants us to understand prayer, and what is needed in our prayers, so that we will be able to pray effectively and have every one of our prayers answered.

We have a promise in scripture that states if we pray, God will answer our prayers. Yet that's not the experience most of us have with prayer. So why doesn't God answer all of our prayers? Prayer is more than getting what we want from God; it is relationship. The greatest blessing that God can give to man is the spirit of earnest prayer. Prayer will do what no power on earth can accomplish. The soul that turns to God for help, support and power through prayer will have the light, the peace, the serenity and the very essence of God manifesting through them.

Just like this excerpt from the gospel writings of Ellen. G White, she explains that 'Prayer is the breath of the soul. It is the secret of spiritual power. No other means of grace can be substituted and the health of the soul be preserved. Neglect the exercise of prayer, or engage in prayer spasmodically, now and then, as seems convenient, and you lose your hold on God.' By maintaining a connection with God through prayer, we will find strength, grace and a continual hunger and thirst after righteousness. Such lifestyle of effectual prayer keeps us in God's will and mighty power; even a brief prayer can bring heavy spiritual power and allow for the miraculous to happen

For all of us, prayers bring the will and blessings of God into our lives. As I am passing through and reflecting on what I've encountered through prayers and with God, so far, all I can say, is that, it has been an amazing and illuminating experience. So therefore I address this to all those in and out of the Christian faith; An outcry to those who have been lost and discouraged in the place of prayer, this is not the time to shy away from it. I encourage you to hold diligently on to your weapon of prayer and boldly use it at every given opportunity, both in good and bad times. God is longing for you to discover your power to avail through prayer.

If you feel that you would like to know Jesus personally and that you would like to have a close relationship with him please read out this prayer below:

Dear Lord Jesus, I ask you to forgive my sins and save me from eternal separation from God. By faith, I accept your work and death on the cross as sufficient payment for my sins. **This very moment, I accept Jesus Christ as my own personal Lord and**

Saviour, according to your Word, right now I am saved. Thank you, Jesus, for dying on the cross for me, redeeming me and giving me eternal life. AMEN.

If you prayed this prayer of salvation and meant it, Congratulations! You are now a follower of Jesus Christ. The Bible tells us that your eternal salvation is secure! "That if you confess with your mouth the Lord Jesus and believe in your heart that God has raised Him from the dead, you will be saved". (Romans 10:9)